Dennis Potter's numerous television plays include *Blue Remembered Hills* (1979), *Brimstone and Treacle* (commissioned in 1975 but banned until 1987) and the series *Pennies from Heaven* (1978), *The Singing Detective* (1986), *Blackeyes* (1989) and *Lipstick on Your Collar* (1993). He has also written novels, stage plays and screenplays.

D0507228

*in the same series*

SCORSESE ON SCORSESE
Edited by David Thompson and Ian Christie

SCHRADER ON SCHRADER
Edited by Kevin Jackson

CRONENBERG ON CRONENBERG
Edited by Chris Rodley

MALLE ON MALLE
Edited by Philip French

LEVINSON ON LEVINSON
Edited by David Thompson

# Potter on Potter

### Edited by
### Graham Fuller

*faber and faber*
LONDON · BOSTON

First published in 1993
by Faber and Faber Limited
3 Queen Square London WC1N 3AU
This paperback edition first published in 1994

Photoset by Intype, London
Printed by Clays Ltd, St Ives plc

A CIP record for this book
is available from the British Library.

ISBN 0–571–17046–3

2 4 6 8 10 9 7 5 3 1

# Contents

List of Illustrations    ix
Acknowledgements    xi

Introduction by Graham Fuller    xiii
1    THE CHILD OF THE FOREST    1
2    THE SINGLE PLAYS
from *The Confidence Course* to
*Cream in my Coffee*    15
3    IN OTHER WRITERS' HEADS:
*Casanova, Late Call, The Mayor of Casterbridge,
Tender is the Night, Christabel*    64
4    SERIALS WITH SONGS:
*Pennies from Heaven, The Singing Detective,
Lipstick on your Collar*    80
5    FILMS AND STAGE PLAYS:
*Pennies from Heaven, Brimstone and Treacle, Gorky Park,
Dreamchild, Track 29, Sufficient Carbohydrate*    105
6    DIRECTOR AND NOVELIST:
*Blackeyes, Secret Friends*    125
7    CONCLUSION    139

Filmography    143
Bibliography    164
A note on the editor    166
Index    167

To Margaret Potter, my steadfast wife

# Illustrations

1 *State Fair* (1945)
2 *The Count of Monte Cristo* (1934)
3 *The Confidence Course*: Dennis Price as the Director
4 *Vote, Vote, Vote for Nigel Barton*: John Bailey as Jack Hay, Barton's political agent
5 *A Beast with Two Backs*: Patrick Barr with the 'culprit'
6 *Son of Man*: Colin Blakeley (centre) as the Galilean rebel
7 *Traitor*: John Le Mesurier, Jack Hedley
8 *Blade on the Feather*: 'visitor' Daniel Young (Tom Conti) and traitor Jason Cavendish (Donald Pleasence)
9 *Where Adam Stood*: the father (Alan Badel)
10 *Where Adam Stood*: the son (Max Harris)
11 *Blue Remembered Hills*: Colin Jeavons, Michael Elphick, Janine Duvitski, Colin Welland, Robin Ellis, John Bird and Helen Mirren
12 *Cream in my Coffee*: Bernard and Jean (Peter Chelsom and Shelagh McLeod)
13 *Cream in my Coffee*: Bernard and Jean – forty years later (Peggy Ashcroft and Lionel Jeffries)
14 *Cream in my Coffee*: Martin Shaw as the predatory singer of cheap songs
15 *Casanova*: Frank Finlay
16 *Tender is the Night*: Peter Strauss as Dick Diver
17 *Christabel*: Newsreel of the Germans entering Paris
18 *Christabel*: Christabel (Elizabeth Hurley) and Peter (Stephen Dillon) – the sidelong glance
19 *Lipstick on your Collar*: 'I See the Moon' (Douglas Henshall, Ewan McGregor and Giles Thomas)
20 *Pennies from Heaven*: Bob Hoskins as the song salesman Arthur Parker
21 *Pennies from Heaven*: Cheryl Campbell as the Forest of Dean schoolteacher Eileen

22–24  *The Singing Detective*: Michael Gambon as Philip Marlow (hospital patient, gumshoe and crooner)

25  *Lipstick on your Collar*: Giles Thomas as Private Francis, the new boy in the War Office

26  *Lipstick on your Collar*: fantasist Private Hopper (Ewan McGregor) and the 'common' Sylvia (Louise Germaine)

27  *Lipstick on your Collar*: Director Renny Rye with Dennis Potter

28  *Pennies from Heaven*: Steve Martin as Arthur Parker

29  *Pennies from Heaven*: Christopher Walken in the 'Let's Misbehave' number

30  *Gorky Park*: William Hurt

31  *The Wizard of Oz* (1939)

32  *Dreamchild*: Alice (Amelia Shankley) with the Gryphon and the Mock Turtle

33  *Dreamchild*: Mrs Hargreaves (Coral Browne) with the Gryphon and the Mock Turtle

34  *Dreamchild*: Producer Kenith Trodd and Director Gavin Millar

35  *Dreamchild*: shooting the Mad Hatter's tea party

36  *Schmoedipus*: Mother and son? (Anna Cropper and Tim Curry)

37  *Track 29*: Mother and son? (Theresa Russell and Gary Oldman)

38  *Blackeyes*: Gina Bellman

39  *Blackeyes*: Michael Gough as the novelist Maurice James Kingsley

40  Dennis Potter directing *Blackeyes*

41  Dennis Potter directing Alan Bates in *Secret Friends*

42  *Secret Friends*: Alan Bates

43  *Secret Friends*: Gina Bellman

# Acknowledgements

The major part of this book comprises interviews with Dennis Potter conducted over four years. The first was made during a transatlantic telephone call on 24 October 1988, at which time Potter was gearing up to direct *Blackeyes* in London. The second interview was in New York on 11 January 1992, just prior to the Museum of Television and Radio's comprehensive retrospective of Potter's television work. Interviews three, four and five were conducted at Twickenham Film Studios on 13, 14 and 15 April 1992, when Potter was supervising the production of *Lipstick on your Collar*. Principal thanks, then, to Dennis Potter for his considerable eloquence and his readiness to discuss his work in detail, often at times of severe physical duress.

Walter Donohue offered not only many invaluable editorial suggestions, but also unflagging support and patience.

The Museum of Television and Radio's Potter retrospective, which moved on to the Los Angeles County Museum of Art as this book was being completed, was a major resource. The curator was Ron Simon, and Diane Lewis and Laura Braunstein of the museum arranged private screenings of Potter's work.

Additional thanks to Sarah Adair, Judy Daish, Robert Geisler and John Roberdeau of Briarpatch Films in New York, Lynn Kirwin, Ted Panken, James Saynor, Ingrid Sischy, Mary L. Smith, Theresa Sturley, David Thompson, Kenith Trodd, Sarah Tuft, Cara White of Clein and White, Rosemarie Whitman of Whistling Gypsy Productions, Jenner Sullivan, and Bobbie Mitchell of the BBC archive.

Stills courtesy of the BFI Stills, Posters and Designs; copyright held by London Weekend Television (*Blade on the Feather*, *Cream in my Coffee*), Whistling Gypsy Productions (*Lipstick on your Collar*, *Secret Friends*), Twentieth-Century Fox (*State Fair*), MGM (*Wizard of Oz*, *Pennies from Heaven*), Orion (*Gorky Park*), Thorn EMI (*Dreamchild*), HandMade Films (*Track 29*). Copyright for all other stills held by the

BBC. Photographs of *Lipstick on your Collar* by Stephen F. Morley.
Photograph of Dennis Potter and Renny Rye by Tony Russell.

# Introduction

'Rules and models destroy genius and art'
William Hazlitt

In January 1992 Dennis Potter was invited to New York to attend a series of seminars on his television plays, the subject of a comprehensive retrospective at the Museum of Television and Radio. He made the trip, somewhat hesitantly, torn 'between the apparently opposing need to be alone with my own being and the equally urgent desire to address what used to be called the public at large', and spoke, in his hypnotic, sing-song and ever so faintly sardonic Gloucestershire burr, of the imperatives that had driven his career. He also made it clear that he finds such mass-scrutinization of his work a soul-taxing experience if he happens to be in the room. At the time, it should be noted, he was undergoing one of his periodic attacks of psoriatic arthropathy, the hereditary illness he has suffered from since he was twenty-six and which he bequeathed to Philip Marlow, the hospitalized hero of his masterpiece, *The Singing Detective*. The third seminar began with a series of clips, among them the cathartic moment in *The Singing Detective* when Marlow, face wet with tears, releases the memory of a childhood trauma and stands up in his wheel-chair as Dr Gibbon starts to lip-synch the words to the Ink Spots/Ella Fitzgerald version of 'Into Each Life Some Rain Must Fall'. As the screen went blank, Potter, sitting next to Kenith Trodd in the front row, stood up himself and walked lankily on to the stage, scarcely able to hold back his own tears. No one needed to inquire whether Potter's illness-racked adulthood had contained such moments of self-revelation. 'I hadn't seen that thing for a while,' he told his interlocutor with understandable self-defensive rancour. 'Can't you tell?'

Profoundly emotional – as we Englishmen tend to be beneath our native phlegm – Potter has spent twenty-eight years ransacking his life for his art, not to regurgitate that life as it was, is, might have been, or could be, but to transform what experiences he has had into an imaginary flight-path into the realms of common, communicable experience. Perhaps it was the shock of seeing Philip Marlow projected on to a big screen that caused Potter's distress, since his approach to writing was originally based on the idea that 'one of the ways of jumping over the hierarchies of the print culture was television, because anyone or everyone could see it'. To this end, Potter continues to write as if he is purging himself: 'To empty myself until I can't carry on emptying myself.' The author of twenty-nine single television plays, four original serials and five serialized adaptations from other writers, and latterly the director or producer of his own work, he has been not only dauntingly prolific but the most important creative figure in the history of British television. Had he written exclusively for the theatre, rather than for a populist medium, he would rank as a major literary figure by now; instead, his reputation has run parallel to television's, and only the cinematization of television drama in the eighties has brought his work into the arena of serious critical study. As Kenith Trodd suggests: 'There's a sense in Britain that any screening or performance before a paying audience enhances the product *by definition* over something like *The Singing Detective*, which is seen by millions on TV. If you can disengage from that snobbery, there are few writers in any dramatic medium who can be compared to Potter.'

Potter's early plays broached the themes that he has continued to explore and define: political disillusionment (*Vote, Vote, Vote for Nigel Barton, Message for Posterity*); England's decay (*The Bonegrinder*) and ongoing social malaise (*Shaggy Dog, Paper Roses*); the role of popular culture (*Where the Buffalo Roam, Moonlight on the Highway*); sexual inhibition (*Alice*) and disgust (*Angels Are So Few*) born of puritanical repression; betrayal (*Traitor*) and guilt (*Stand Up, Nigel Barton*); the interplay between past and present, truth and fiction, reality and imagination; and the need for every human being – from Nigel Barton and the Al Bowlly disciple in *Moonlight* to Casanova, Jesus, Marlow and *Blackeyes*' Jessica – to understand his or her identity. His vision is profoundly religious in its yearnings – indeed, he has frequently taken his structures and metaphors from the Chapel teachings he received as a child – despite avidly renouncing the prescribed placebos of organized religion. In Potter's writing, god (but not God) is always in the details – not a deity waiting in the wings to absolve man of his sins, but a promise of redemption, of wholeness, for those who seek to know themselves by gathering up the fragments of their shattered psyches. A graduate of Sunday school as well as Oxford, Potter has been described by Julian Barnes as 'a Christian socialist with a running edge of apocalyptic disgust', but if he ideologically endorses neither Christianity nor Marxism, his writing grows out of a matrix of the two, resulting in a deeply felt, humanistic optimism. To understand that optimism, though, often requires a leap of faith and the acceptance that it might take the devil to rape a catatonic girl out of her stupor, that a sexually bored housewife, oppressed by a canting husband, might summon an angel into her bed one dull suburban afternoon, that what traditionally passes as 'good' might contain the seeds of 'evil' or vice versa.

More even than his beloved Forest of Dean, the landscape Potter occupies is the inside of the head. Where other writers have been constrained by the dramatic parameters of the 'here and now', Potter has trade-marked a number of bountiful and profoundly unsettling techniques for navigating the streams, tributaries, cross-currents and sewers that flow through his protagonists' minds. Challenging viewers' assumptions about what they are watching, he pioneered the fourth-wall-breaking, anti-theatrical techniques of non-naturalism – more out of necessity, he says, than design – and at times has provocatively utilized the noisome imagery of misanthropy and sexism, often returning to a passage of writing, as if he needs to exorcize the sentiment behind it. Thus a comedian contemplating his sister's imminent death from cancer feels reflex-ive revulsion at the sight of a Pakistani sweeping up a pile of muck on the floor of a fast-food joint in *Joe's Ark*, a detail turned into a misogynistic anecdote in *Blade on the Feather*; a disgusted meditation on the 'sweaty farce' of human conception in Potter's novel *Hide and Seek* is revisited, almost word for word, in *The Singing Detective*. Potter has reworked and reinvestigated entire plays – *Alice* as *Dreamchild*, *Schmoedipus* as *Track 29*, *Lay Down Your Arms* in *Lipstick on your Collar* – but the mood of the new work is always unnervingly different from that of the first. The assiduous Potter-watcher will even find a troubling word still troubling a decade later: questioning his own use of 'vouchsafe' in the introduction to a collection of his plays published in 1984, Potter unearths the same archaism in *Lipstick on your Collar* in 1993. If that sounds like *Mastermind* trivia, or no more than an author's recurring verbal tic, it also signals Potter's continuing engagement with the 'tyr-anny and treachery of words which are dependent upon education, which in itself is dependent upon class in England', the very subject of *Rain on the Roof*. 'I think any writer has a small field to keep ploughing,' Potter says, 'and eventually you turn up the coins you want.' He is a writer who has also turned his ploughshare inwards, writing caustically about the omnipotence, or impotence, of writers, in drama after drama.

Looked at as a whole, Potter's plays might be regarded as a twenty-eight-year Swiftian discharge of bile – 'I cont abide dirt. It d'get everybloody-where, doan it?' says young Philip – but it is that very act of discharging that leads his characters towards a state of ultimate grace.

It is fair to say that no other living English television dramatist or screenwriter has created such a diverse, coruscating, yet intellectually rigorous and thematically consistent *oeuvre* as Potter has in the two *Nigel Barton* plays, *Moonlight on the Highway*, *Son of Man*, *Traitor*, *Follow the Yellow Brick Road*, *Brimstone and Treacle*, *Joe's Ark*, *Double Dare*, *Where Adam Stood*, *Blue Remembered Hills*, *Blade on the Feather*, and *Cream in my Coffee*. Then there is *Casanova*, and the two great serials with songs, *Pennies from Heaven* and *The Singing Detective*. Not all Potter's efforts have been successful in conception or execution. He is a rather cold novelist, self-consciously concerned with form, unin-terested in telling stories. With the exception of *Dreamchild*, his feature films pale beside his mature television plays. In 1989 the *Blackeyes* serial, his *Rashomon*-like grappling with the brutalizing effects of the objectifi-cation of women, earned him the harshest abuse of his career, and rapidly dwindling audiences. To make matters worse, it had been his first project as director. If the Hazlitt quotation that sits at the top of this introduction is a handy epigrammatic touchstone for a survey of Potter's seditious disdain for naturalism, there is an unlooked-for irony in that word 'models', for few critics looked beyond the fashion model Blacke-yes' exposed nipples, soft-core mugging and blank stare, into the heart of Potter's self-taunting, post-feminist inquisition. If the public was alien-ated, it was probably less because of moral outrage than the fact that Potter's sculpted cinema of ideas – in itself a discomfiting aesthetic for a television audience craving nothing more radical than *Neighbours* or *The Darling Buds of May* – was too much like something they would try to avoid at the National Film Theatre. *Secret Friends*, the film which fol-lowed *Blackeyes*, with Potter again at the helm, was another weird mix-ture of the demotic and the abstruse. But if by 1992 Potter seemed out of synch with the 'common culture', *Lipstick on your Collar*, the third part of his song-cycle, promises an exact realignment.

Any up-to-the-minute appreciation of Dennis Potter as an *auteur* straddling both films and television is complicated by the fact that the vast majority of his work has been done for the domestic medium. Since the late seventies, the disappearance of the studio-based TV play has pushed him gradually towards movies. Until the advent of Channel 4's Film on Four series and other television companies' move towards film production in the eighties, the two media were perceived as discrete channels of communication with differing vocabularies and mandates. Potter thrived so long as a television dramatist because the studio-based play in which he served his apprenticeship was, like all televisual experiences, a verbal medium drawing on its own codes, clichés and communal history. Although he shifted expediently into all-film productions with three superb plays for London Weekend Television in 1980, he feared that the passing of the electronic studio would usher in the era of the anti-literate, style-oriented TV movie director, as has been borne out by the poor crops of recent small-screen drama. Potter's own ultra-stylish direction of *Blackeyes*, with its arty décors and swooping, predatory *plein air* camera movements, only contributed to the sense that a new, hybrid form had emerged – with one problematic foot in the enclosed (and threatened) world of television drama and the other in the wide open spaces of cinema.

Interestingly, it is in America, a country long starved of indigenous quality television, where Potter has found his most appreciative audience in recent years. Virtually an unknown quantity there until *The Singing Detective* was aired on a few PBS stations in 1988, his tardy canonization came, none the less, with a reluctance to accept that the serial was the work of a television writer, as if that somehow devalued it. '[Potter has] made writing for television respectable and, possibly, an art,' declared Vincent Canby in a rave review in the *New York Times* that was accompanied by the headline 'IS THE YEAR'S BEST FILM ON TV?' Joseph Papp's Public Theater, which had previously provided a showcase for *Dreamchild*, was duly awarded a D. W. Griffith Award by the National Board of Review for bringing the serial to the big screen, and an attempt was made by members of the New York Film Critics' Circle to honour it as a theatrical film; several senior critics, among them Andrew Sarris and Richard Corliss, included it in their top ten films of the year. This is all very well, but *The Singing Detective* was written, designed and directed as a television programme. To regard it as otherwise is a crucial misunderstanding not only of Potter's aspirations as a writer, but of the televisual history that shaped him and his work. To the casual observer it may seem unimportant whether Potter writes, directs and/or produces for television or film or both; however, the uneasy alliance between the two media suggested by the American misappropriation of *The Singing Detective* for the movies and the art-house *mise en scène* of the BBC's *Blackeyes* not only affects critical responses to his work but raises the rather more pressing problem of where Potter, nearing sixty and in the late afternoon of his career, now positions himself in a Britain facing up to a deregulated television industry and with no film business to speak of. If at times he seems unstoppable, the rest of the nineties will none the less be a difficult time for him.

As it relates to Potter, then, the word *auteur*, used as a catch-all buzzword for directors in popular movie journalism, is clearly unhelpful; it is only marginally less so in its proper use as a term applied after the fact by film scholars. Just as clearly, there is no figure working in British film and television today who has so persistently addressed his own themes and preoccupations, who has so indelibly customized his own methods, or who is so worthy of a book in a series devoted to *auteurs* speaking about their own work. He was hesitant about the project himself at first: 'I suppose it's worth it, this, isn't it?' There is, of course, the matter of record, the long overdueness of such a book, and, not least, the compelling way Potter articulates his passions in the following interviews (with, I should add, the bullish modesty he demonstrated that evening in midtown Manhattan). And, at a time when the very notion of adventurous British screen drama – film and television – seems to be sinking into the sea, there cannot be too many reminders of the vertiginous heights attained by its finest practitioner.

Graham Fuller
November 1992

# CHAPTER I

# The Child of the Forest

'When I grow up, *everything* . . . Everything ool be *all right* . . . Won't it? Won't it, God? Hey? Thou's like me a bit – doosn't, God?'

Philip Marlow, age nine, in *The Singing Detective*

As will become clear, the subject of this book is no respecter of biographies or questions about the autobiographical content of his work. His life, though, feeds his writing to a probably abnormal degree, and certain salient facts are inescapable. Dennis Christopher George Potter was born on 17 May 1935 in Berry Hill, Gloucestershire, England, the son of Walter Potter and his London-born wife Margaret, who would later have a daughter, June. They lived with Potter's paternal grandparents in a four-room stone cottage. Like most of the local men, Potter's father and grandfather were coalminers who worked the pits of the Forest of Dean. This ancient royal forest of oaks and ferns, grazing land and orchards, small coalmining communities with their Free Church chapels and working-men's clubs, lies between the rivers Severn and Wye, just east of the Welsh border. It is the Arden of Potter's childhood and as suggestive a psychic landscape in his work as Monument Valley is in John Ford's Westerns. There is, however, no correlation between the sentimentally depicted boyos of Ford's Welsh epic *How Green was my Valley* and the weary, fractious miners of Potter's *A Beast with Two Backs* and *Pennies from Heaven* or the psilicotic 'grancher' of *The Singing Detective*. The Forest represents Lost Eden in Potter's work, the site of sins original and unoriginal: a married miner, taunted by his mistress, batters her to death in *A Beast with Two Backs*; children of the Forest turn on the weakling among them, and he burns to death in a barn, in *Blue Remembered Hills*; Arthur Parker seduces the virgin schoolteacher Eileen in her stone cottage in *Pennies*; young Philip witnesses his mother's adultery among the briars in *The Singing Detective*.

Apart from a spell in treeless Hammersmith – its iron bridge is the scene of Arthur and Eileen's final reconciliation and the trench-coated Marlow's hardboiled musings – Potter's childhood was happy, if not without incident. He has spoken of his betrayal of a classmate, echoed in *Stand Up, Nigel Barton* and *The Singing Detective*, and in the introduction to *Waiting for the Boat* (1984) he wrote of 'something foul and terrible that happened to me when I was ten years old, caught by an adult's appetite and abused out of innocence'; children are sexually abused in the plays *Moonlight on the Highway* and *Where Adam Stood*, in the novel *Hide and Seek*, and in the novel and series *Blackeyes*. Potter has admitted to having been a 'pale, timid, and precocious child, not too badly bullied', though his cleverness and the approval of his teachers singled him out from his contemporaries and invoked his reclusive tendencies. On passing the Eleven Plus in 1946 he attended Bell's grammar school, Coleford, and won a scholarship to St Clement Dane's grammar school in London. Following National Service in 1953–5 he went up to New College, Oxford, in 1956 to read Politics, Philosophy and Economics, also on a scholarship. At Oxford he acted in student plays and discovered his natural ebullience as editor of *Isis* and chairman of the Labour Club.

Potter was part of a meritocratic movement among intellectual young working-class men and women in England in the late fifties, and like his fellow television playwrights Alun Owen, Arnold Wesker and David Mercer, he would come to agonize about it. In 1958 Potter was interviewed for a television programme after writing an article about class mobility in the *New Statesman* and, as Alan Sinfield reports in *Literature, Politics, and Culture in Postwar Britain* (1989), 'his remarks were taken up by the Labour paper *Reynolds News* under the headline "MINER'S SON AT OXFORD ASHAMED OF HOME. THE BOY WHO KEPT HIS FATHER SECRET" '. In 1960 Potter added grist to the mill with his scathing treatise on contemporary England *The Glittering Coffin* and in 1961 with *Between Two Rivers*, a documentary he wrote and presented about the Berry Hill community for the BBC.* As late as 1965 he was still railing against his experiences as a scion of the working class. 'The

---

* 'Everything I saw began to take on depressing and drab colours,' he said on camera. 'The forest came to narrow and constrict itself around me. The fortress became a prison. Even at home with my parents, I felt a shame-faced irritation with the tempo of a pickle-jar style of living . . . I loathed the thought of lives and minds warped by the dirt, clay, and mud of such filthy working conditions. I could see no virtue in grubbing in earth for a living. And I thought then that this miserable pile of dull villages could not possibly be reconciled with great art, great thought, vital emotions, and classical music . . . And now, after a number of years, I find myself back with a shining new degree and looking at these drab, untidy old houses which once seemed to me to be the expression of all my dislike and frustration, and I find myself wondering.'

days of the timid, kow-towing little runt of a scholarship boy are long since over,' Nigel Barton tells his upper-class girlfriend in *Stand Up, Nigel Barton*. But that play is also a working-out of anxiety and of Potter's feeling that he may have betrayed his origins in the documentary. It was also the first of many Potter plays to explore the tension between fathers and sons, although it would be an oversimplification to suggest that the source of that tension is purely Oedipal. There is no more heart-felt line in all of Potter's work than Philip Marlow's lament for his 'lovely, dear old Dad', written some ten years after the death of Potter's own father in 1975.

After Oxford, Potter joined the BBC as a general trainee and worked on *Panorama* and with filmmaker Denis Mitchell, and under Grace Wyndham Goldie in the Television Talks Department, for whom he made *Between Two Rivers*. His forthright articles in the political press, disapproved of by the BBC, steered him towards newspaper journalism. In 1961, while working as a feature writer for the *Daily Herald*, he suffered the first symptoms of psoriatic arthropathy, a hereditary illness that had afflicted his maternal great-grandfather and would attack Potter's mother when she was widowed in her sixties. A chronic skin disease that ossifies the joints (both Potter's hands are permanently closed fists) and causes the body to lose control of its temperature, inducing hallucinations, it recurs in three-month spells two or three times a year. It turned Potter into a virtual recluse until the mid-seventies, when he was first treated with the anti-cancer drug Razoxane, which was subsequently discovered to have carcinogenic side-effects. He now controls the illness with Methotrexate and Etretinate.

Invalided in his mid-twenties, unable to get around, Potter became the *Herald*'s acidulous TV critic, but he was able to stand, unsuccessfully, as the Labour candidate in the Conservative stronghold of Hertfordshire East in the 1964 general election. After a month as a leader writer for the broadsheet *Sun* (into which the *Herald* had mutated), Potter resigned in October 1964. Shortly afterwards he developed a novel he was writing into the script for his first television play, *The Confidence Course*, which was shown on BBC 1 in February 1965. A trenchant television critic, highly dismissive of 'anodyne' entertainment and American imports, he continued to contribute to the *New Statesman*, was a regular critic on the *Sunday Times* from 1976 to 1978, and has written a number of acerbic articles about the parlous state of British television for the British tabloids.

In 1959 Potter married Margaret Morgan, a 'green-eyed dazzler' whom he'd met at a dance and whose father was also a Forest of Dean miner. They live in a Victorian house in Ross-on-Wye – where Potter does most of his writing, overnight and in longhand – eight miles from his birthplace. They have three grown-up children, Sarah, Jane and Robert. An accomplished all-rounder for England's women's cricket team, Sarah is also the novelizer of her father's play, *Brimstone and Treacle*.

GRAHAM FULLER: *Do you remember when and how you first learned to read?*

DENNIS POTTER: I think I learned to read in the chapel before school – Salem Chapel, which was a little stone, square, free church. The preacher preached to the working man. It was a bit like Methodism, but slightly less structured than that. In Sunday school there you would start to pick out words before you went to school at the age of five. My feeling is that words began to make sense and take shape via things like Sankey's *Sacred Songs and Solos* and the verses of the hymns – exactly 1,200 hymns in a little floppy, orange-covered book, which were quite simple, because, I suppose, it's an evangelical Christianity. They were about crossing the Jordan and meeting people on the other side, or 'Come hail or storm or flood'. They were both simple and dramatic. There was a vividness, too, in the King James Bible and particularly in the New Testament – the parables.

I learned these hymns in surroundings that were not so different from what they described: the Forest of Dean, which is between the rivers Wye and Severn in the west of England, bordering on Wales, is very hilly, with ugly, working-class villages but beautiful, stony landscapes. It is a genuine forest which you can genuinely get lost in, which creeps right up to the little miners' cottages. When I was a child, by far the biggest source of employment was the coalmines. My father was a miner, and everybody I knew in school – apart from the odd shopkeeper's son, or the children of people who worked in quarries or the forest – would have been coalminers' sons and daughters.

The combination of that landscape and the tight, almost suffocatingly close, working-class culture with the imagery of those evangelical hymns or the wonderful language of the Bible provided a whole series of metaphors. My first impulses to actually see words make sense in sequence came out of that combination.

As a child – aged four, five, six or seven – it is natural to see the surrounding landscape as the landscape one reads about. So I thought of the big ponds near the pit where Dad worked as Galilee. The Valley of the Shadow of Death was a lane descending between overhanging hedges where you tended to want to whistle – but I was a timid child anyway, and the forest itself was a labyrinth of old oaks and beeches and ash trees. The words both of those hymns and the Bible, and fairy stories, too, fitted very happily into that landscape.

The speech of the area is a very strong regional dialect. 'Thee' and 'thou' is the most common way of saying 'you'. You would say, 'Where'st thou going old butty?' instead of 'Where are you going pal?' or whatever. It's a very old English. You would say 'highsht' for 'hist', meaning 'listen carefully', and 'surry' – 'Where'st thou been, surry?' – from 'sirrah', of course. The Forest of Dean is forty-odd miles from Shakespeare's native patch. That kind of English speech comes naturally to me and its rhythms creep into my most tender moments. Whenever I wished to be tender with my children, when they were very small, I would say 'thee' and 'thou', as my father did to me.

GF: *The fathers in some of your plays – for example, in* Stand Up, Nigel Barton *and* Lay Down Your Arms – *do not encourage, or are suspicious of, reading and bookishness. In* Traitor, Where Adam Stood *and your film* Secret Friends, *fathers drill reading or learning into their sons, and sequester them from natural joys and play. The young Edmund Gosse in* Where Adam Stood *doesn't even know who Robin Hood is. Your paternal grandfather, I know, couldn't read. What was your own experience of reading in your parents' home?*

DP: I once said, in a would-be casual aside in an interview many years ago, that my father had only read one book in his life, and that, I think, was by Hall Caine. Such a remark, in an English class situation, appears to imply some kind of condescension or patronizing contempt, which was not the case at all. My father was very proud of the fact that I seemed to be bright and could draw and write. He used to put some of my drawings up on the mantelpiece, and then tear them up if he thought I was getting too uppity. He himself, when describing the past, would almost casually describe the colour of the sky and how he felt that day. And he would always draw an apple or something on the white margins of the newspaper.

Of course, the English class system – I don't mean British, because it's not the same in Scotland and Wales – is so strong, so innate, instinctive almost. I grew up in a wholly enclosed coalmining community, which is geographically isolated as well; in sophisticated metropolitan terms you could even call it 'backward'. At school I was very good at exams. I had a high IQ, and teachers who, although they weren't class traitors, tried to inculcate us with a love of reading books and of learning, and so I started to pull away – willy-nilly, I began the process of judging my background. Then that terrible English thing creeps in at the edges – a kind of complicated shame about the way you speak, the fact that there are no books in the house, and you make assumptions about your family. You are too young to deal with that, but the guilt comes much later. When I started writing Dad was still alive – I was living about ten miles away on the edges of the Forest of Dean – and I think he got to the stage where he was shy with me: he would lean on the door-jamb when I was in the middle of something and say, 'Bist thou all right, old butt?' And I'd say, 'Yes, thank you, Dad.' I wanted to carry on writing. 'Are you sure you're all right, now?' 'Yes, thank you, Dad.' And he'd hover a bit and say, 'Well, good to see thou at work.' It's too late, but if only I could now say, 'Come on in. Just let me put my pen away. Let us talk.' But one always has a continuing relationship, even with the dead. As someone said, 'Our souls are the same parish.' I feel I definitely have a continuing relationship with my father.

Of course, what I was doing – my exams, going up to Oxford – all that was alien to him. He had the constant fear that I wouldn't be like the other boys in the village. But it was inevitable I wouldn't be. You can't journey through forty-seven different classes – as George Orwell would have put it – because of your brightness, without compromising yourself in some way, without inadvertently committing a series of subtle betrayals, for which you eventually pay the price. If you cross frontiers from the ages of, say, eleven to sixteen, then you are going to get tangled up about what you think you're gaining without realizing what you have lost. This is not something I think an American would understand – not in quite the same way that it is understood in England.

GF: *Don't you think America has a different kind of class system?*
DP: Yes, but it's based upon money and race, perhaps, less so than it used to be, but certain rigidities remain.

GF: *Did your mother encourage your imaginative side? There's the story that she was once aghast to find you writing hymns, when you were still very young.*
DP: I have just one memory – I suppose I must have been about six – of a rainy day. I was sitting on the window-sill, looking down at the garden sloping down towards the earth-closet at the bottom, and watching the

rain run in rivulets down the path. I remember trying to write something about the rain, but the images came in the shape of a hymn, because that was my experience of how you put words together. My mother probably thought it was a complicated form of blasphemy – not that either of my parents were religious in that sense; they just, in their matter of fact way, assumed a basic Christian background, unexamined and possibly unfelt. Ultimately, I think it was the fact that it was odd for a six-year-old to phrase words in this way, and with rhymes, even though the rhymes were like Sankey's or Moody's hymns – or Wesley's if I was being really ambitious!

So I just remember the rain pattering on the window-sill, and asking, 'Mum, Mum, what shall I do?' Of course, this was during the war, and getting hold of paper was a huge problem. The idea of having sheets of clean paper on which to write would have been glorious to me.

GF: *You moved with your parents to London when you were ten – as nine-year-old Philip does with his mother in* The Singing Detective.

DP: My mother was a Londoner, so in one sense she was outside the Forest of Dean culture. Even now – she's eighty-two and still lives there – she's still half thought of as an outsider, after fifty-eight years. But she made that attempt to escape. Dad wanted to get out of the pit, but you weren't allowed to change jobs if you were a miner. The idea was that he would be allowed to follow us to London on compassionate grounds, but they wouldn't let him. We came back after nine months. I wouldn't eat; I wanted to go back to the Forest of Dean. Although most of the kids at school had been evacuees during the war and had been to the country-side, they hadn't been anywhere like the Forest of Dean, and when I'd say things in this uncouth 'thee–thou' language they'd look at me strangely.

GF: *You lived in Hammersmith?*

DP: Yes, Rednall Terrace, a street on what is now the London end of the Hammersmith flyover. It's gone now, just as the school I went to has also disappeared. The school was right next to St Paul's Church. Now there's a road going right through it and they've dug up half the churchyard.

GF: *From seeing* Pennies from Heaven, *we know that as a child you were exposed to popular music on the radio, but do you remember the first films you saw?*

DP: There was a cinema in Coleford in the Forest of Dean, and when I was very young they were showing heroic war films. I saw one film about aeroplanes. I don't remember its name, but I remember afterwards, getting on the bus, I wanted to be a pilot. When we lived in London I used to go to what is now called the Hammersmith Odeon – that huge cinema on Hammersmith Broadway – but it was then the Gaumont. I thought it was a palace, and I was impressed that the films were shown continuously, so you could come in in the middle. People *did* come in in the middle, and watch until it came round again, and then they'd clap up their seats and say, 'This is where we came in.' But I just sat there the whole time, if I could!

I can clearly remember the first time I went to the Gaumont, when I was ten. It was some time between VE Day and VJ Day. The second feature was a Dagwood Bumstead and Blondie film, and *Tarzan* was the main feature. Outside the cinema they'd put up the names in eight- or nine-foot letters, and I thought it meant they could only ever show those films, and that they'd put those letters up in honour of the greatest films ever made! Then, again in 1945, I saw *State Fair*, in colour on a huge screen, with Dana Andrews, the pig and Dick Haymes singing in the swingboats at the funfair. In fact I used a song from it, [Rodgers and Hammerstein's] 'It Might as Well be Spring', in *The Singing Detective*. I thought seeing that film was the most wonderful experience anyone could possibly ever have. The cinema was an Art Deco, thirties kind of place. I remember it had two big pyramids of light: the transparent curtains used to rustle open and then the projector beam would go *boing!* and hit the screen, laced with blue tobacco smoke. And you would see the organist, and the tip of a great, white, gleaming Wurlitzer – I think it was a Hammond organ actually – rising like a demigod out of the pit. The totality of that experience was something I will never forget.

GF: *Did you have a particular fondness for musicals?*
DP: No. Just for those pictures flickering on the screen. I used to get nightmares from them as a child, that was the trouble. My mother stopped me going. When I saw *The Count of Monte Cristo* I didn't sleep for a week because of that man with his tangled beard in the next cell, who'd been in prison all his life and scraped little holes in the wall. The terror of that affected me deeply. I'd wake up covered with sweat, thinking I was in that cell. Films have the effect of totally occupying your sensibilities.

GF: *Your work deals with all the ages of man, but – except in* Where the

1   *State Fair* (1945)
2   *The Count of Monte Cristo* (1934)

Buffalo Roam, Rain on the Roof *and* Sufficient Carbohydrate – *you haven't dealt much with adolescence and the teen years.*
DP: No, I haven't. I don't know why that is and I don't know if it's significant. *Lipstick on your Collar* basically deals with an eighteen- or nineteen-year-old National Serviceman who is emotionally a fifteen-year-old, and that's probably the closest I've been to that age-group.

GF: *Between school and Oxford, from 1953 to 1955, you did your own National Service in the army. In both* Lay Down Your Arms *and* Lipstick on your Collar *you depict a callow young soldier arriving at the War Office in Whitehall just as the Suez Crisis is about to unfold. By the time Suez was happening, you yourself had gone up to Oxford, but I imagine that people watching* Lipstick *will make the same kind of 'autobiographical' assumptions as they did about* The Singing Detective.
DP: People do make these assumptions, which amuses me greatly. I use apparent autobiographical forms because I find that they're very powerful; it's the dramatic equivalent of the first-person novel. I use the surface details and the knowledge of places, or, in the case of *The Singing Detective*, illnesses. But it isn't about *me*. What I do isn't autobiographical, but I like dramatically the feeling that it is. That's not a cheat. It's simply a method of appearing to inhabit one person's head in a 'truthful' way. You're saying, 'This is what happened,' but it isn't. The truth one is really trying to get at is something other than that, which would take a long time to explain.

Autobiography is the cheapest, nastiest, literary form; I think only biography beats it. It's very interesting that they are the two most popular literary forms at the moment. Novelists who try to write in the first person are taking the autobiographical mode as their model, and I frequently, but not always, do the same. The authenticity of the background and the surface detail is therefore guaranteed, as is the emotion, which gives me the licence to introduce and explore emotions that are *not* mine, that are fiction.

I am not writing my life story, but I am aware that I am *living* a fictional life in a way. When my illness first hit me, I was full of disappointment: I was drowning on the *Daily Herald* and various guilts were bubbling and slowly seeping through. I thought, 'The only way I can save my life is to invent my life.' I hope I'm not being immodest, but I think there is a certain emotional power in my work which I become aware of *later*. And I think that power is actually the result of the contest between my real self and my invented self. My invented self overcomes my illness

– which has been a considerable burden for thirty years, and the treatment of which is almost as bad as the illness itself – and keeps me sane. Well, sort of sane.

GF: *When you left Oxford you became a graduate trainee at the BBC and wrote and did on-camera narration for* Between Two Rivers, *a 1960 documentary about the mining community in which you'd been raised. In your* Arena *interview with Alan Yentob in 1987 you admitted culpability for what had been a rather patronizing appraisal of your origins. Do you still feel that it was a betrayal?*

DP: Yes and no. I was unwise enough to express what I felt at that time without filtering it through the sensibilities of the people I was portraying. If that's a betrayal, it was a betrayal. But it's a more complicated betrayal than the word suggests. I don't *know* I betrayed, full-stop, and in that sense I didn't. The betrayal was in not making it fiction – a most important lesson.

GF: *Without fictionalizing it, you couldn't have access to a metaphor or an objective correlative.*

DP: There was no metaphor. Also, it's a function of fiction to tell truths, and we've lost sight of that. Documentaries don't tell the truth, as I saw myself when I made one. They show you what is there, but they don't mediate it through the truths of all the complications, all the inner subtleties of why this person is like that, why that person is like this. Documentary is simply naturalism, simply observing behaviour, with a voice-over telling you what you're supposed to think. Whereas fiction, drama, films, plays, all avoid that form of dishonesty – or *can* avoid it. They don't usually, I know. But that's what drama's for, to tell truths.

GF: *What were your first attempts at drama?*

DP: I worked for a year, in 1960–1, on a Sunday book programme on the BBC called *Bookstand*, for which I dramatized excerpts from novels. So I had some familiarity with the form. When that came to an end I joined the *Daily Herald* [as a feature writer] on August Bank Holiday 1961. On my first day I sat between one old man who was writing Readers' Letters and another old man who was writing the Stars. Around this time I also did a few sketches with David Nathan, a colleague on the *Daily Herald*, for *That Was the Week That Was*.

GF: *You showed that grubby, thankless world of tabloid journalism in*

*Paper Roses, in which you made the garrulous old human-interest reporter, played by Bill Maynard, both pathetic and sympathetic. Did you base that character on one of your colleagues?*
DP: Yes, there was a man who talked and talked and talked and talked. He'd say, 'My boy, never write *over* a number, never say "over 200 people". As old Lord Northcliffe used to say, "What do you mean over? Hang it over their heads." It must be *more than* . . .' And everyone would say, 'Oh, for God's sake, shut up!'

GF: *You were at the* Herald *when your illness first struck in 1961. Do you recall that vividly?*
DP: I knew something physical was going to happen, and it did. That particular day I was covering the Young Conservatives Conference, of all things, on the Euston Road. I hated being there. I hated having to file that copy. I remember I went to get up from the press table, and I couldn't. I looked down, and my left knee was the size of a soccer ball, bulging out against my trousers. I was already very pale, and I had some odd patches on my neck and on my arm, but I didn't know what they were. Then the arthritis, which they took some time to diagnose because of the weird swiftness of it, just invaded every joint – bang! My jaws, fingers, knees, hips, ankles, toes. And paralysis became more than a metaphor for how I felt about my job. It was actually sitting in me; that's what it felt like.

Shortly after that, just as quickly, overnight, my skin went. And I thought, 'Well, this is it, then.' What I wanted to do, or what I *thought* I wanted to do – to have a political career, to be a public man – wasn't possible. But all of a sudden, there was a whispering seduction within that despair, saying, '*Now* you can do whatever you choose. *Now* you don't have to go out and fend in that way, with those people, about those things.'

It took some time to start writing, but that was the breeding ground for it. And the invention of the self became a fundamental physical necessity for me. At the same time came the knowledge of what the so-called significance of my life was supposed to be. The two things came together. Now you could say that my illness was psychosomatic, except that psoriatic arthropathy is a genetic condition. It's just that I had reached such a low point that for various reasons the affliction was also a release.

GF: *You describe it almost like an epiphany, or a visitation.*
DP: It was like one of the plagues of Egypt! With 100 per cent psoriasis you lose control of your body temperature. You semi-hallucinate. You're

in danger of septicaemia, and therefore you're in danger of dying. People say they've got psoriasis, and they mean they've got some really uncomfortable itches, which don't hurt and don't make the skin flake off. With the extreme psoriatic arthropathy that I have you can't find a point of normal skin. Your pores, your whole face, your eyelids, everything is caked and cracked and bleeding, to such a degree that without drugs you could not possibly survive. It was physically like a visitation, and it was a crisis point, an either–or situation: either you give in, or you survive and create something out of this bomb-site which you've become – you put up a new building. That's what it amounted to.

GF: *You have referred to your illness as your 'shadowy ally'. I assume you mean it created by default the conditions in which you could write. But did the illness affect every aspect of your life?*

DP: It's bound to have affected everything since it came crashing in thirty-two years ago, when I was twenty-six. I've been ill for more than half my life, and certainly for the greatest part of my adult working life. It was sufficiently chronic and severe to have affected everything I do. I can't even imagine now what the young man was like who didn't have it. I remember playing rugby and things like that, but I can't now conceive what that was like. I have long since lost that sort of regret. I no longer think, 'Oh, if only it would go away.' It's controlled with drugs and I can manage.

GF: *Even with this affliction, you went on to stand as a Labour Party candidate in the general election of 1964. Was Nye Bevan the politician who inspired you the most as a young man? I ask this because you insert footage of Bevan speaking about the Suez Crisis at Trafalgar Square in* Vote, Vote, Vote for Nigel Barton.

DP: If I could single out one such figure, it might well be Bevan. He had wit and passion, and a tremendous style, which was capable of invoking great loyalty amongst his followers.

GF: *Did you identify with the New Left?*

DP: To a degree. They were interesting in the sense that they rejected Stalinism and all that aspect of left-wing politics. They were opening new jars, finding new lids, but they were very ideologically driven as well, and it was that pattern of voting the ticket – even though it was an intellectual one – that became oppressive, emotionally and intellectually. I always kept one foot outside the circle.

GF: *What, then, was the desire behind your decision to stand for Parliament?*

DP: That was simply what I wanted to do, and what I thought, at Oxford, I should be wanting to do. It was on the trajectory of my thoughts, ambitions, feelings and fears. But physical problems intervened, I think fortunately so, because I was growing uncomfortable with my political role, even though it was a self-determined one. By the time I stood for Parliament I was already carrying a walking stick, and the combination of my illness and my sense of withdrawal from a belief in the kind of Britain I would have preferred to see meant that I was no longer satisfied with such a role: it wasn't creative enough, it didn't satisfy me. I simply didn't fit the bill in the end. Although I was a Labour candidate I didn't even vote in that election. I was probably the only candidate who didn't vote for his party.

GF: *You didn't vote for yourself then?*

DP: No. I realized this wasn't what I felt, it wasn't what I was *for*. It's odd – it may even be a form of mild insanity – but I had always felt that what I did was going to have some significance. I was aware that there was a vocation, but I didn't know what it was. My disappointment with working on the so-called Labour newspaper, the weirdness of the 1964 election, the crisis of illness, the feeling of failure, the intense despair – all this made me feel blocked and empty. I felt a kind of entropy of the emotions. When I lost the election, I couldn't go back to the *Herald*, which by then had mutated into the pre-Murdoch *Sun*, though in those days it was still a broadsheet paper owned by the *Daily Mirror*. The need to re-create myself coincided with finding the way to do it, which was through drama. I could have gone the 'theatre' way or the 'novel' way, but something – maybe the guilt and anxiety about the gap between my origins and what I had become – steered me towards television. The palace of varieties in the corner of the room.

# CHAPTER 2

# The Single Plays

From *The Confidence Course* to
*Cream in my Coffee*

'It's the *plays* that do all the damage. The plays.'
Jack Black in *Follow the Yellow Brick Road*

Beginning with *The Confidence Course* (1965), Dennis Potter wrote nine of his first fourteen television plays for the BBC's Wednesday Play series and a subsequent five for Play for Today. Like ABC's Armchair Theatre series, the Wednesday Plays broke from the theatrical traditions of early British television drama and provided a window for writers to experiment in form and style. 'It reached towards the extreme limit of an inevitably self-conscious swing away from filmed theatre,' Potter wrote. 'Despite its excesses, the series injected new life into the almost moribund television play. It encouraged many writers to believe that it was once again possible to work without too much frustration in television.' (In the same essay* he maintained that 'by 1964, the general policy of the BBC appeared to have moved against the survival of the full-length single play'.) Potter would, of course, become the most celebrated exponent of 'non-naturalism', but he wasn't the sole advocate. In 1964 Troy Kennedy Martin, whose hard-edged scripts for the police series Z-Cars had challenged the cosiness of the long-running *Dixon of Dock Green*, wrote a manifesto in *Encore* decrying naturalism in British television drama and co-wrote with John McGrath a series called *Diary of a Young Man*, which used still photographs and a weirdly accented voice-over narration. Other writers, such as John Hopkins and David Mercer, experimented in hyperrealism, yet the era is best known for its prevailing naturalism and gestures towards social realism – such as Jeremy Sandford's *Cathy Come Home*, and other Ken Loach/Tony Garnett films – to be followed in the seventies by the socialist realism of Trevor Griffiths and Jim Allen.

For all his methods of dramatizing 'the inside of your head' and use of

---

* From Introduction to *The Nigel Barton Plays* (1967); see Bibliography.

direct address, Potter knew when to turn to an externalized, linear narrative. Dealing with rural insularity, *A Beast with Two Backs* (1968) is a
realistic parable of religious faith gone astray in the Forest of Dean of the
1890s. *Son of Man* (1969), Potter's Passion play, trades not in miracles
but in biblical realpolitik, and features an angry, persuasive and loving
Jesus who has more of the shop steward about him than the Messiah. It is
actually less religious in tone than the series of 'visitation' plays that
Potter wrote in the early seventies (*Angels Are So Few*, *Only Make
Believe*, *Schmoedipus*, *Brimstone and Treacle*), in which angels,
assassins, devils and demiurges are called up by the emotionally repressed
or housebound as a source of liberating violence or sex, as if in answer to
a prayer. The visitation motif is also used in *The Confidence Course*,
*Moonlight on the Highway* (1969), *Joe's Ark* (1974), *Pennies from
Heaven* (1978; in the person of the door-to-door salesman who calls on
Joan), *Blade on the Feather*, *Rain on the Roof* (both 1980) and *Secret
Friends* (1992).

Potter eschewed the idea of political drama *per se* but looked askance
at the spiritually bereft world of party politics in *Vote, Vote, Vote for
Nigel Barton* (1965), and at the cultural ramifications of treason in
*Traitor* (1971) and *Blade on the Feather*, the first inspired by Kim Philby's exile in Moscow, the second – an acerbic pastiche of the Le Carré
spy-thriller genre with a Tolkien-like don at its centre – completed
shortly after the announcement that Anthony Blunt was 'the fourth man'.
Two of Potter's finest plays, they are ambivalent, non-ideological studies
of England's historical decline and the sense of melancholy that attends
it.

Perhaps Potter's greatest single plays, though, are those that engage the
audience in an imaginative discourse about what it is they are seeing, and
obsessively probe the collaborative act of making and watching television. In *Follow the Yellow Brick Road* (1972), a paranoid actor
(Denholm Elliott), cuckolded by his wife (Billie Whitelaw) and humili-
ated in the television commercials he appears in, can't shrug off the
camera that follows him around like a malignant god. Potter uses the
character ironically, having Jack denounce television drama – 'it's the
*plays* that do all the damage' – and praise the commercials as a repository
of hope and purity and love. This piece, brilliant in its skewed self-
reflexivity, mordantly shows how human aspirations are commodified
into quasi-religious blips, rather like Arthur Parker's cheap songs in *Pennies from Heaven*. Similarly, in *Double Dare* (1976), a physically sick,
blocked writer (Alan Dobie) who has a morbid, repressed love for an

actress (Kika Markham), casts her as a prostitute in his unwritten play, using this salacious scenario to pour out his disgust for her traitorous participation in a phallic chocolate-bar commercial. Almost a psycho-thriller, it 'doubles' its characters, anticipating *Pennies from Heaven* (Arthur's *doppelgänger* is the epileptic Accordion Man), *Dreamchild* (the young Alice Liddell and the octogenarian Alice's teenage companion), *The Singing Detective* (the two Marlows), *Blackeyes* (Jessica and Blackeyes) and *Secret Friends* (Helen as wife and call-girl), among others.

Potter's work was instantly controversial. *The Confidence Course* brought the threat of law suits from the Dale Carnegie Institute. Written before its companion play *Stand Up, Nigel Barton, Vote, Vote, Vote for Nigel Barton* was originally telerecorded in March 1965 and scheduled to go out in April. The tape was damaged and the play re-recorded for June transmission, but the prospect that Potter's caricaturing of fusty Labour traditions and pompous Tory speechifying might irritate party representatives meant it finally didn't go out until a week after *Stand Up, Nigel Barton* that December, and then not without alterations that 'disfigure the play in a few important ways'. In fact the play is more about the ingrained lying that preserves institutionalized politics and the effect that has on the idealistic Nigel (Keith Barron) than an attack on any ideology.

There were further moans – from within and without the BBC – about Potter's swipe at Churchillianism in *Message for Posterity* (1967) and his 'hippie' Jesus (Colin Blakeley) in *Son of Man*. Although Potter had stepped outside the BBC to make *The Bonegrinder*, *Shaggy Dog* (both 1968), *Moonlight on the Highway* (1969), *Lay down your Arms* (1970) and *Paper Roses* (1971), it was the banning of *Brimstone and Treacle* by the then BBC Director of Television Programmes, Alasdair Milne, in 1976 which drove him out of the Corporation's arms.* Potter and Kenith

---

* Potter delivered *Brimstone and Treacle* to the BBC in 1974 and it was accepted for production, with Kenith Trodd assigned as producer and Barry Davis as director. It was scheduled to appear on Play for Today on BBC 1 on 16 April 1976, the second part of an informal trilogy with *Double Dare* and *Where Adam Stood*. Bryan Cowgill, controller of BBC 1, viewed the programme, recorded just prior to transmission, and recommended several small changes, which were implemented, and a later time slot, as well as advance warning to viewers about the play's content. Cowgill reportedly referred the play to Alasdair Milne, who found it distasteful and had Cowgill withdraw it from the schedule, despite a preview feature on the plays having been printed in the *Radio Times*. 'I found the play brilliantly written and made, but nauseating,' Milne wrote to Potter. 'I believe that it is right in certain instances to outrage the viewers in order to get over a point of serious importance,

Trodd, a friend from army days and the producer most associated with Potter from *Moonlight on the Highway* through *Christabel*, were further offended when the BBC paid them just a format fee for brokering a serialization of Anthony Powell's *Dance to the Music of Time* novels. The break came when Potter was asked to write six 75-minute plays for the BBC and in December 1978 was told that they would have to become 'five 50-minute' plays instead, or Trodd's contract would be cancelled. In 1979 Potter and Trodd formed an independent production company, P.F.H. Ltd and negotiated a deal with Michael Grade at London Week-end Television for nine plays to be filmed under P.F.H.'s artistic control: six by Potter; *The Commune*, a two-parter by the *Spongers* team of writer Jim Allen and director Roland Joffé; plus a work by an unan-nounced writer. The deal was a fillip for British independent production companies and the terminally depressed film industry, and anticipated Channel 4's future role as a television 'publisher'. In the event Grade terminated P.F.H.'s contract when *The Commune* exceeded its £790,000 budget by £35,000, and the three completed Potter plays – *Blade on the Feather*, *Rain on the Roof*, *Cream in my Coffee* [1980] – ran over their total budget of £832,000 by £150,000, although Trodd argued that LWT's notion of film costs had been unreasonable to begin with. Exas-perated with British television, Potter announced his departure for Holly-wood to work on the screenplay of *Pennies from Heaven* for director Herbert Ross. In the eighties Channel 4's Film on Four and the BBC's Screen One and Screen Two series replaced the single play on British television. Apart from *Visitors* (1987), a film version of *Sufficient Carbo-hydrate* (1983) for Screen Two which lacks the conviction of the original stage play, Potter's television work since 1980 has all been in serial form.

The tapes of three Potter plays – *The Confidence Course*, *Message for Posterity* and *Shaggy Dog* – have been wiped, while *Emergency – Ward 9* (1966; its hospital scenes prefigure those in *The Singing Detective*) was transmitted live and never recorded. Their absence is a testament to the lack of seriousness accorded television authorship in the sixties.

———

but I am afraid that in this case real outrage would be widely felt and that no such point would get across.' Milne did not specify which were the offending scenes. Potter sought an injunction to have his name taken off the other two plays and wrote an article in the *New Statesman* on 23 April 1976 condemning Milne's 'brief and insolent letter', the BBC's methods at large, and its waste of the £70,000 of licence-fee money which had been spent on the production. The banning coincided with a wave of censoriousness at the BBC during the mid-seventies; Quentin Crisp's *The Naked Civil Servant* and Brian Phelan's *Article 5* were also banned. *Brimstone and Treacle* was finally aired on BBC 1 on 25 August 1987, by which time it had already been produced as a stage play and movie.

GF: *How did you first transmute into a writing career the despair you felt about your illness, your departure from the* Daily Herald *and the end of your political ambitions?*

DP: I remain sufficiently a Christian to know that despair is, in the old words, a very great sin. My first television play was called *The Confidence Course*, and I now understand, in retrospect, why and how it came about. It is really about the self-motivation courses run by bodies like the Dale Carnegie Institute, which I covered as a newspaper reporter at one of their so-called free sessions. The *Herald* wouldn't use the article because Dale Carnegie was advertising in the paper.

A group of people gathered together in a hotel conference room – some of them were planted, I believe. The speakers were hustling and bustling people up to the front, where they'd let them speak for three minutes, then describe how they could have done it better, how they should impress people – standard pop psychology. They'd show you how to have a better memory by blindfolding somebody who would recite a list of twenty objects that they'd just seen. I thought this was so theatrical – an attempt to pull certain kinds of social skills out of people – and phony. I was just there as an observer, because of the piece I was writing, but I could see it was like chapel again, except that the chapel was *about* something. It used a series of vivid metaphors to give a perception of purpose, beauty and danger – they were perilous metaphors, too. What interested me was why those people were there, what sort of anxiety had brought them to that hotel. But something deeper was worrying me about it, and that was this so-called confidence factor. This was about self-functioning at a time when I was beginning to feel that I couldn't self-function. The people running it were saying, 'We can give you confidence.'

GF: *In* The Confidence Course *you invoke the figure of the early nineteenth-century essayist William Hazlitt as a disruptive stranger. I notice that you refer to Hazlitt, perhaps more than any other writer, in interviews and conversation. It made me wonder if he was the most profound literary influence on your own work.*

DP: I think Hazlitt's argumentative, springy, rhetorical essays represent the peak of a certain kind of English prose. He was an odd combination of very progressive – to the extent that we still haven't caught up with him – and quite reactionary. He would prefer an old book to a new book, an old thing to a new thing; you also see that, though I think to a lesser degree, in someone like George Orwell.

3  *The Confidence Course*: Dennis Price as the Director

I am interested in the tension in oneself between an instinct that cherishes order, tradition and discipline, and what, in general terms, might be called a concatenation of right-wing emotions underneath or interlaced with radicalism, where your mind tells you other things. This tension – which I think is evident in Hazlitt and Orwell – is intrinsically dramatic, because it means you're on your guard against the facile optimism and brutal idealism of the left, even though intellectually you respect and indeed share in it; at the same time, you pay due attention to the things that would normally be called 'right-wing'.

Coleridge and Wordsworth made the journey within their own lives from an adulation of the French Revolution to a kind of High Toryism. And there is that element in the Conservative Party which I quite respect – that Old Tory, Dr Johnson element, if you like, as opposed to the canting humbug of the left. Obviously I could never bring myself to vote Conservative, and I suppose it would be accurate to say that I am on the left, but many of my feelings are what would commonly and crudely be called right-wing. Emotionally, I believe the greatest danger to the human race is lack of order. That doesn't necessarily imply a sanctioning of hierarchies, but it does imply a belief in law. It's complicated. I deliberately don't write explicitly about politics because I prefer the tension between these two poles within myself – what in Marxist terms would be called a dialectic, I suppose – to be implicit. I don't like political drama because I think the way to argue politics is through the essay or prose discourse. Obviously your feelings and aspirations – social, religious and political – inform what you write. But I don't think you should write on their behalf; you shouldn't fly those flags.

GF: *No, but all characters, because of their social background, their aspirations, are perforce political.*
DP: Yes, they can be, but if you don't set out to make them representatives or mouthpieces for this or that ideology or political stance, you retain the possibility of surprising yourself about how complicated they are. For example, the Denholm Elliott character – I suppose he is the villain – in *Brimstone and Treacle* is so far to the right that he has subscribed to the National Front. And yet, as I was writing him, he recoils when the idea of real evil, of the consequences of his thought, is put to him by the visitor, and in the act of recoiling manages to say things like, 'All I want is the England I used to know . . . I just want it to be like it used to be.'

That sort of idiotic nostalgia has profound emotional springs for people, as you can see now with the break-up of the Soviet Union. It is too easy to dismiss those collections of feelings as stupidly right-wing or fascist. Human beings are more complicated than that; their aspirations are curiously entangled with the past and with this nostalgia.

GF: *You've said that nostalgia is a second-order emotion. That implies that the past is inevitably a bitter or painful place.*

DP: It's not so much that it's bitter or painful, because it's also a very funny and tender place. The thing about it is that it isn't necessarily behind you, but can, if you turn the corner, be standing fully armed and implacable in front of you. There's an obsession with the minute-by-minute sensation, with what you think you are now, but by definition 'now' is just the last few seconds of decades of experience. Nostalgia is a means of forgetting the past, of making it seem cosy, of saying, 'It's back there – look how sweet it was.' But you can use the power of nostalgia to open the past up and make it stand up in front of you. This is why I use popular songs. Often the initial reaction is, 'Oh, how sweet to hear that thing again!' but then the very syncopations can bear in things that have been knocked away by the present and that are important, that tell you what you are, why you are doing what you are doing, and why every act that a person does has some sort of significance. The ripples never quite die away.

GF: *Do you think there's a danger in looking back sentimentally at the past?*

DP: I think it's necessary for human beings, that they *have* to do it, but that to make the past a sentimental enclave is a psychologically danger-ous thing to do. The object of mental health is to have in balance all that has happened to you and all that you strive for and want to do – in other words, to understand yourself; that's true of religion, and of psychiatry. Mature, balanced individuals have to have regard for what they came from, are, remember, did, wanted, to be able to measure what they are.

If nostalgia is pressing a button and conjuring up a twee, Technicolor version of the so-called past, then it *is* a second-order emotion. An ache for what cannot be reclaimed is technically infantilism. The past isn't safely tucked away. Psychoanalysis or your own memory will tell you that what made you in the wider sense – your own culture, your own language, your own communality which you shared with your forebears – is actually shaping the future, too. It's people without a sense of the past who are alienated and rootless, and they're losers; they lose out.

To make any political statement you first of all have to know who and what you are; what shaped your life, what is possible and what isn't. That's not nostalgia. That's a kind of grappling with the past – an ache for it, perhaps, sometimes a contempt for it. But the past commingles with everything you do and everything you project forward.

GF: *Do you think that applies to national psychologies too? To the English psychology?*

DP: To a degree, in that our culture – and I don't mean by that flags and drums and soldiers and stamping boots but the long, slow rhythm of a culture – clearly shapes the responses of the people who have shared that culture over the centuries. And that's what I am most aware of, through its absence, in the United States, although there are versions of it in those hyphenated Americans: Italian-Americans, German-Americans. You don't often hear of British-Americans or English-Americans, maybe because we were the dominant shaper in terms of the language and so on. But the long, slow rhythm of a place, a people, a language – a shared history – is bound to create things in common that you don't even recognize until they have been wrenched away. But even when the lid is still on, under it are old ghosts, and something very minor can easily lead to fascism. I'm not talking about nationalism or patriotism. There's a profound difference between that and acknowledging a shared culture, which I think is important to any writer – perhaps more important than to most others.

GF: *In* Stand Up, Nigel Barton, *Nigel pontificates about his humble origins – the pits and working-men's clubs – in a television programme about class, and enrages his father, who has spent all his life in that environment. He tries to explain, not very convincingly, that the pro-gramme was badly edited, but his father is not appeased. Did you write the play as an apologia to that culture and to atone for* Between Two Rivers?

DP: In retrospect it does look like it. But it is and it isn't – that's the only way I can tackle it. This question constantly recurs. People say, 'That was you, wasn't it?' or, 'That's you discharging that guilt,' or, 'That's you reliving that particular event.' There is some truth in that, but it's also *not* the truth, not what those particular scenes in the 'Nigel Barton' plays were about; they were as much about objecting to the way politics was presented on the screen as about my own discharging of guilts. Using the guilt as a dramatic device is not discharging it. There is no way you can

discharge guilt. What is, is. What you've done, you've done. What you've
lived through, you've lived through. You cannot bend the knee and say
*mea culpa* and ask for the past to be wiped away. But you can use guilt. I
don't mean by exploiting it, but that you can live within it and *show* it,
which is the only possible form of absolution. It's not a case of, 'I am
guilty, therefore forgive me,' but of reinhabiting the guilt in order to
understand it.

GF:  *Did your father see* Stand Up, Nigel Barton?
DP:  Sure, and he was very proud of it. He was proud of everything I did
– that was the nature of our relationship. He was a gentle man and
he loved me. That knowledge will continue. As I say, it's an ongoing
relationship.
  I also realized at the time of the 'Nigel Barton' plays why I had chosen
television. You could say it was a form of absolution again, that dream of
the possibility of a common culture – a dream that I no longer have
because it's not tenable. But the pull within me was very strong and I
used to express it in just such canting terms. The thought that dons and
coalminers would watch the same programme at the same time, as, of
course, they did. I came from people who wouldn't open a book, who
wouldn't go to the theatre, and who didn't go to the cinema all that often
either. But there is that thing in the room, showing stories and pictures,
jumping right over the hierarchies of our print culture. And although
television still expressed English condescensions and the English class
system, and was timid and smug at the same time, it was an arena that
drew me because of *where* it was, how it was and what it could do.

GF:  *Having failed to get into Parliament and having turned your back*
*on newspaper journalism* . . .
DP:  Having *succeeded* in *not* getting into Parliament, you mean!

GF:  *Well, the fact that you didn't vote for yourself suggests you didn't*
*really want to be an MP.*
DP:  No, I didn't.

GF:  *Did you then see television drama as an alternative way of attacking*
*the ills, the inequities, you saw in British society?*
DP:  No. It was more a tearing away from the public person I'd been. I
had no wish to duplicate that party political rhetoric as a writer. One
system of discourse cannot be described in terms of another. We're talk-

ing about utterly different things that have an utterly different grammar. At no point did I sit down and say, 'I am going to address this or that social evil.'

GF: *But it came out anyway, in play after play.*
DP: It would come out, yes. Whatever it is that makes one want to seek political change must be part of one's view of the world. The purpose of my writing was not to express that view, but the view was within me, and obviously my way of seeing the world comes out. There's the danger that writing about politics can lead to didacticism and preaching. I think there are other and better ways to approach those things. Drama – for want of a better, less pompous word – is, in all its forms and manifestations, the last area that can still deal with the world without seeming to apply a bandage to it or introducing a political programme. It doesn't say, 'Look at this injustice.' It may be doing all of those things, but that's not its purpose.

GF: *Is that why you haven't tackled Thatcherism, or even Majorism, per se?*
DP: I do, but not in that preaching way. I think politics in the wider sense, and religious aspirations in their wider sense, are very much part of what it is that makes a person function or not function. But to say A leads to B, would be to write a political essay. In fact, I started out writing such things. My first publications and my first aspirations were entirely political. But necessity, as it were, turned me in upon myself, and I was grateful for that turning-in.

GF: *One could say that people like Arthur Parker in* Pennies from Heaven *and Philip Marlow in* The Singing Detective *are products of the society, the political climate, in which they live.*
DP: They are certainly products of their time, their environment. The narrowness of their hopes, their yearning, is realistic in that sense. But beyond that I wanted to show the way Arthur's cheap songs were representing something else, something we all have, which can easily be stifled. The fact that he couldn't manage it, that he was weak and blown off course by every little tune, as it were, is characteristic of most people. It's true whatever régime people live under or by or through.

GF: *You have, none the less, had urgent things to say about party politics in* Vote, Vote, Vote for Nigel Barton, *about Churchill in* Message for

Posterity, *and about class divisions in many of your plays. I'm pursuing this because I want to know what was the impetus behind your decision to write television drama.*

DP: Well, 'television' because it could speak to everybody, and 'drama' because I discovered that that was what I not only wanted to do, but *could* do. It was my path toward finding myself, redefining or inventing myself again. It *was* me. You are getting close to that sort of ganglion, those nerves, whatever it is that make one person utterly different from another – it's impossible to put into words. I can see all sorts of connections between one piece of my work and another. All kinds of half-hidden images and metaphors, links in the chain. And in many ways I'm writing the same thing over and over again; I know that. But it is not for me to get too close to why I do it. I don't want to threaten the source of what I do, and why I do it. I don't sit down when I am writing and think, 'It's about this,' or, 'I am attacking that,' or, 'I am addressing this or that issue.' It doesn't feel like that, and therefore it cannot *be* like that.

The kinds of questions I do ask myself are: Why did he say that? Why did she say that? What is it that they didn't say when they said that? What is the hidden text of that conversation? What is each person thinking? What is inside those two heads, if it's a scene between two people? What is his past and her past? What does he want? What does she want? It doesn't feel like writing an essay. It doesn't feel like making an argument. It doesn't feel like having a purpose. It feels like something you knew but didn't know you knew. It feels like dreaming. Sometimes you get that sense of *déjà vu*, and then you say, 'I've been here,' or, 'Surely you've said that before.' That slightly creepy, prickly feeling that there's a script. Or a memory will come plunging at you through an old piece of music, however banal, or through a smell, or a shape. The way a room is patterned will remind you of another room, one you haven't thought about in thirty or forty years.

Writing is like that. I never have a plot. I don't have a schema. I want to know what's happening. I want to know why. But I don't do it *because* I want to know why. I'm doing it, and *then* I want to know why.

GF: *Do you rough out stories?*
DP: No.

GF: *You just start writing?*
DP: I either have one image, or I may have a sense of where the image has got to be, and then find that it hasn't got to be there at all, which is

4　*Vote, Vote, Vote for Nigel Barton*: John Bailey as Jack Hay,
Barton's political agent

always the best feeling. Then I write – and I write extremely intensely, hour upon hour until I'm exhausted, because I'm frightened of losing it when I'm doing it. I hate starting it, too. I hate the *process*.

When you're doing it, it's a bit like a dream, but a troubled dream – the kind of dream you want to wake up from, although not a nightmare. But the intensity of the experience is such that you are almost receiving what you're writing. Of course, you're shaping it at the same time, and then you add to it also. It's an odd thing, knowing that a scene has got to come to an end, or that you've got to make a turn. You don't know what it's going to be, just that you *must* – then it's done. It's being on a trip. It's being subject to it as well as controlling it.

GF: *Do you always write in a linear fashion, from Scene One?*
DP: From the starting point to page 17 or so, yes. Then I usually destroy all those pages and start again.

GF: *Are you a copious rewriter?*
DP: Only when I'm in difficulties. Normally I write very fast. I wrote *Dreamchild* in four and a half days, probably because I'd occupied that territory before with *Alice*, in 1965.

GF: *In that play the young Alice Liddell splashes water in the face of the Revd Dodgson/Lewis Carroll. It seems to me to be an overtly Freudian act of sexual mockery, sexual betrayal.*
DP: It could be, but it's also simply a little girl splashing water in order to push away an adult's too-intense stare; a sort of primitive stirring of awareness that his attention upon her was too strong for her to deal with. But also, in the simple, childish way of mockery, mocking the solemn, and then not realizing the extent of the hurt. But labels like 'Freudian' aren't that helpful, because a scene isn't built that way, in my head, when I'm actually writing it. The retrospective view – why something worked or didn't – is the critic's function. Maybe to use labels is inappropriate. People dream up all sorts of connections between, say, two plays that are separated by several years, where no connections exist, or fail to make them when they do. At least, they may be there subconsciously, but they are not there deliberately. Those assumptions are always dangerous.

GF: *But what about something like* Schmoedipus, *which is knowingly informed by the Oedipus complex and ideas like regression to childhood?*

DP: Yes, but *Schmoedipus* simply grew out of that Jewish joke, 'Oedipus, Schmoedipus, what does it matter so long as the boy loves his mother?' Obviously, any piece of work of any value or worth will be capable of being interpreted in those psychoanalytic terms. People who inhabit the Freudian terminology or a very strong political ideology or religious structure can always pick any piece of work, even one diametrically opposed to their beliefs, and feed into it their preconceptions. Drama is very open-ended that way. You only have to look at the different ways you can interpret any play – maybe the author went against the grain of it, maybe he went with it, maybe he made it gay, maybe he made it political. Look at the different ways people interpret Shakespeare. In other words, you can read so much into a work. But as the writer, the more consciously you seek that kind of terminology, the worse the play. I've said in the past that the closer writing becomes to any kind of therapy, the worse it is; the closer it approaches an ideology, the worse it is. The more open-ended it is, the more those ideologies and beliefs and superstitions of contemporary intellectual fashions can vibrate within it, then the more capable it is of absorbing interpretation, because it's working as a *drama*. If it didn't work, it wouldn't lend itself to such interpretations.

Going back to *Alice*, you can see the 'splashing water' scene simply as a cruel child threatened by a too-fixed stare, or simply a child being mischievous, *or* you can say, 'Ah, the water is a symbol.' All of those interpretations are perfectly feasible. And in the last resort, whatever's delivered, it's not for the writer to interpret.

GF: *So you bring what you know and what you don't know to a piece?*
DP: Yes. Often what you don't know is bubbling away there, clearly – the feeling you get when you know a scene is working. Obviously not all scenes work, but every now and again you reach a place where you have that glow. Your pen is gliding away, and you feel everything fits, all the different elements are cohering, all at the same time. When you're writing like that it seems the only way to do it. But then such apparent certainty in turn becomes permeable to all sorts of interpretations. Even when I use cheap songs, as in *Pennies from Heaven* and *The Singing Detective* and *Lipstick on your Collar*, the same is true. The sugary banality of those tunes and lyrics is unspecific – bad art is unspecific. Popular art in general is unspecific. But the unspecific nature of it allows you to put in the specific. Now good art, if there is such a thing, is specific. You write a scene and you feel, if it's good, that it's actually, concretely, the only way

those people could have behaved in that situation – but it also has some
of the openness or looseness of popular art.

GF: *Right from the start of your writing career you had adults dressed as
children in* Stand Up, Nigel Barton, *and characters addressing the camera
in both 'Nigel Barton' plays. Did you feel that the naturalistic television
drama of the day was restrictive?*

DP: Not just the drama – everything on television. They used to call it
'the window on the world', as though you were looking out at reality.
And the whole grammar of television is based upon that assumption, that
you are just looking at things, and those things are real. But I think
television lends itself – as you see in commercials now – to a totally non-
naturalistic treatment. Unfortunately, that commercial style has invaded
drama – it's very difficult now to tell what is and what isn't a commercial, but you know you're being sold something.

I cannot work in a naturalistic mode. It's not the way I think, and I
don't think it's the way other people think, or remember, or express their
emotions. And to use non-naturalistic devices in a naturalistic medium is
a way of making people put the lights out, draw the curtains, sit around
and pay attention. If it fails, of course, it fails – abysmally. If it works, it
works in a way that draws you right into that box, as opposed to standing looking through a window, which is the way it usually is.

All writers are aiming at a sort of realism. But naturalism assumes that
the world out there is *as it is*, and I know that not to be the case – and
most people know it. If they really examine themselves they know that
their own feelings, their aspirations, moods, memories, regrets and
hopes, are so tangled up with the alleged reality of the out-there, that the
out-there is actually interpenetrated by *feelings*. Naturalism can easily
lead to the assumption that you are created by the out-there and by all
the imperatives of the world. Non-naturalism and its use of the inside of
your head is more likely to remind you about the shreds of your own
sovereignty.

GF: *Do you feel there's something non-confrontational about naturalistic drama?*

DP: It gives you what is alleged to be reality – and a reality that cannot
be changed. If you say something is real you say something 'is', and
therefore 'ought' to be. That gap between 'is' and 'ought' is where non-
naturalism lives. Where naturalism can only preach by saying, 'Isn't this
disgusting? Look,' or, 'Isn't this wonderful? Look,' non-naturalism can

subvert. It doesn't necessarily show, or tell, even, but it pulls you in and then turns you inside-out. It's not exactly making you think, but it's making you feel. It is *around* you, it's sensory, it's virtual reality, it's having a helmet on your head, it's cybernetic space – that's non-naturalism!

GF: *It suggests there's a correlation between the television set in the living room and the television set that's on our shoulders, our medium for looking out at the world. It's a hard notion to get around.*
DP: But it can work. It can reach out, that's the point. That's what I believe. That's what I assume to be the case.

GF: *Did the BBC baulk at your initial use of non-naturalistic devices, and, later, when you had characters lip-synching cheap songs in* Pennies from Heaven?
DP: Yes, there was a lot of resistance. Small wonder, really. But even my own producers objected. Ken Trodd wanted to cast children in *Blue Remembered Hills*, and he begged me not to do *Pennies*. The head of drama at that time said, 'What do you mean, they sing? They sing in *every* episode?' 'Oh, yes.' 'But they don't really sing.' 'No.' 'Oh, I see.'
    All that would go on. And then *Vote, Vote, Vote for Nigel Barton* was pulled on the day of transmission and shown some nine months later instead because the BBC was worried about negative reactions from the Labour Party. There have always been lots of little fights and tussles. Things got easier as my reputation grew, though in a way they started getting more anxious about it. More recently, Channel 4 were frightened to death of my directing *Lipstick on your Collar* in case I subverted my own work. And they may have been right!

GF: *In* Message for Posterity *were you implying that the Churchillian breed of statesman was an archaic national monolith?*
DP: There was an evasion going on; the main character should have been called Churchill. But at that time it wasn't possible to write like that – at least, that's my impression. I do remember being very disappointed with the play because it had to be heavily cut to fit the Wednesday Play slot. I'm very glad I didn't carry on with that style. Although you can say, in *Traitor*, for example, character X is like Kim Philby, or Y is like somebody else, those are resonances more in the viewer's mind or in the public domain; they are just allusions. *A Message for Posterity* took a few hesitant steps down a path that came close to being explicit –

polemical, overtly political; it's a legitimate strand of writing, but not one I am really comfortable with or wish to pursue.

GF: *The tape no longer exists, of course. Was it a naturalistic play?*
DP: Yes, basically it was. And if you start writing like that you are pulled into naturalism, to the outsides instead of the insides of the head. Really it was a remnant of soap-box political rhetoric.

GF: *Was* Cinderella *the first of the plays you submitted that didn't get made?*
DP: I think it was. It wasn't very good. The scenes weren't really worked out. I don't think the script survives anywhere. Prince Charming in it was an emotional cripple, ugly and twisted in some way. To be absolutely honest it's very remote in my mind. But it was using a fairy-tale as the given structure, and the search for the bride, i.e. if the shoe fits – all that kind of thing. I think they were probably justified in not wanting to do it, because it was too blatantly using a given myth–tale–story, call it what you will, in order to explain the casual cruelty of fairy-tales – for example, the Ugly Sisters. There's a basic, archetypal, pattern to fairy-tales that lends itself to story structures where you can examine what is actually going on. But I don't think I did that, or certainly not very well. I was annoyed with the BBC at the time, because it's always good policy not to let them get away with anything. But it's best forgotten.

GF: *Was it to be in costume?*
DP: That would have been one of the things to work out, and it would have been interesting. The only scene I recall was set in a very long room, with the ugly Prince Charming slavering and shuffling his way towards the shoe-fitting of the most beautiful girl; there was something sexually repellent about it. There was also a bit too much bravado going on in it; I hadn't digested it, in other words. Because you can use those archetypal structures in a totally hidden way, so that nobody is aware of them.

GF: *Gareth Davies was your main director in those early days and he was still directing your plays as late as 1970. How involved were you in rehearsals and casting?*
DP: At that stage, not very much. I went to read-throughs. I was very ill a lot of this time. Not only that, I was also becoming more and more reclusive. I would go up to London for the one day, and stay overnight, but then my skin was so bad it became as much a social problem as

anything, like leaving layers of your skin in a hotel bedroom. That was a stage when I wouldn't acknowledge it. Anyone with a serious skin illness is usually very loath to talk about it. They try to use every stratagem or device to hide it. I've talked to dermatologists about this, and a lot of chronic dermatological patients are either alcoholics or depressives. Your skin is your outer self – your boundary between you and the world – and inevitably you feel part of that leper syndrome, you know, 'Ring the bell and shout "unclean".' I sometimes used to see people recoil when they saw my hands were psoriatic. Sometimes I had to wear gloves, but the signs of it are so evident that you can't really hide it, even if your instinct is to do so.

GF: *In light of your turning director with* Blackeyes *and* Secret Friends, *had it bothered you not being there when your early plays were being filmed?*
DP: If you've seen my scripts, you'll know they're quite precise and explicit; the stage directions are very full. They are blueprints, in a way. I would talk on the telephone to the people making them and I would go to read-throughs and make some comments – I would then just hope for the best.

GF: *Were you happy with the results?*
DP: On the whole. Sometimes there were problems. My own later impulse to direct them myself was both a function of my being more in control of my physical health through new drugs, and more in control psychologically because I recognized my reclusiveness for what it really was. There had been disappointments about the way some things had been realized, about certain layers within the scripts that were never brought out, and could have been.

GF: *After seven plays for the BBC you did* The Bonegrinder *for Rediffusion and* Shaggy Dog *for LWT. Why did you go outside the BBC at that time?*
DP: I can't remember really. I think that was immediately after *Cinderella* and there was some peevishness going on somewhere. But also I think I had been approached to do something and I was just filling the slot. Every now and again there was a patchy relationship with the BBC or with somebody there, or there was some kind of 'Yah! Boo! Sucks!' thing going on. It may have been one of those occasions – I wouldn't be surprised.

GF: The Bonegrinder *was the first time you'd really examined the clash between English and American culture.*

DP: *The Bonegrinder* was a sure sign of ignorance, in a way, because my illness, and other things, prevented me leaving England until 1977, when I was forty-two. You can write out of prejudice or you can write out of knowledge. I was lying there one day thinking I didn't even know who owned England now, but I was aware of the spirit and weight upon it of American popular culture. I think *The Bonegrinder* is a shoddy, unthinking piece of work; it's there as mere prejudice. But that's the great thing about drama – mere prejudice is shown up for what it is. And if it comes from the writer, then it's well nigh worthless.

GF: *In the sixties and early seventies you wrote plays about tabloid journalism* [Paper Roses], *business practices* [Shaggy Dog], *and about television commercials commodifying spiritual ideals* [Follow the Yellow Brick Road]. *Through all that work there is a caustic appraisal of the media-dominated world. Did you see that as a time of particular spiritual malaise in Britain?*

DP: I don't know. Is it any different now, with the mind and the culture increasingly dominated, in a sociological sense, by a widening technology, increasing media activity, the possibility of the public and the private collapsing into each other and of the public being defined entirely in commercial terms? It represents a really advanced shift in human culture. There was a time when you could shut out that world simply by shutting your front door, but of course that's no longer even remotely the case.

GF: *In* A Beast with Two Backs, *set in the Forest of Dean in the 1890s, the villagers exorcize their collective guilt by uniting against a weaker enemy – in this case, a dancing bear. It's strongly reminiscent of Thomas Hardy, and later, of course, you adapted Hardy's* A Tragedy of Two Ambitions *and* The Mayor of Casterbridge *for television. Was it your own memories of growing up in the forest community that inspired* A Beast with Two Backs?

DP: Yes, there was a local story, from the Forest of Dean, dating from the 1890s about a dozen or so local people who fought with a dancing bear that had mauled a child, until miners returning from the afternoon shift stoned it to death. Several people were arraigned at Gloucester Assizes. It was a story I had heard as a child, and it worried me, because it made me look around me. It was a bit like the Hartlepool people who, in the early nineteenth century, found a monkey on the beach, thought it

5    *A Beast with Two Backs*: Patrick Barr with the 'culprit'

was a Frenchman, and hanged it. The poor bloody monkey was tried by
the local JP, and because it jabbered they thought it was speaking French
– they must have thought Frenchmen looked like that! They didn't literally think it, but *emotionally* they thought it. It shows more graphically
than almost anything you can think of how isolated they were. So
interned were they, they slaughtered the stranger.

GF: *A Beast with Two Backs was mostly shot on film. Did that open new
corridors for you, or did you fear even then that the studio-based play
was under siege?*
DP: I knew it was under siege. It was obvious. You only had to look
inches ahead to see what was going to happen. *A Beast with Two Backs*
was rather curious. It was such a bleak tale. Formally speaking, the
dialogue was less important. Because it was shot on film I tried to use
that to explore the claustrophobic setting of the forest, the woods, the
tiny huddled village of stone, the chapel, the sense of isolation and in-
turnedness – which is a bit like using a studio. I was making that transition, in a sense quite deliberately, to seeing how the alleged freedoms of
film – which can, of course, be a licence to say nothing – could be used to
get the same intensity that a weekend in the electronic studio could give
you. I don't know whether it worked as such, but every now and again it
did reach a kind of claustrophobic emotional power, and the bleakness
within it. Bleakness can be a honourable thing at times; when you strip
things down to their bleak core you can sometimes find something working, some yeasty thing.

Unfortunately I don't think it actually did show the true nature of the
forest, rising in layers between the two rivers – green, black, green,
black, huddled, interned. Some of it didn't get across. But it was a good
transitional phase.

GF: *Were you consciously taking that anecdote of the dancing bear and
using it as a metaphor for something that was in your mind at the time?*
DP: I began with the anecdote, something I'd known since I was small,
not really realizing it was a metaphor. Again, we're going into that
territory about what you know or don't know when you're writing.
Obviously your own intelligence and your own passions, your own con-
victions and beliefs, the things that reverberate for you as an individual,
are going to come out, but that's the right way round. You see, if I had
*begun* with it as a metaphor we could only talk about it in those terms
afterwards. If you talked about it beforehand, you might make the meta-

phor more explicit, but neither you nor the audience would find out anything; you'd end up with what you started with. Generally speaking, that's my main objection to didactic drama, whether political or religious. Of course when a piece is finished you might go back and say, 'Oh, I see what I meant,' or, 'I see what that part of me must have been trying to say,' and then make it clear. But if you started like that I think you would make it didactic, you would preach and teach. Something in the drama itself would have slipped away. It would have eluded your reach because you would have put the net around it too quickly or too soon.

Some of my feelings about the Forest of Dean were coming out in *A Beast with Two Backs* – though at an angle. In that sense the bear stood for the thing that had to be destroyed, the thing that I had sometimes felt as a child about being too clever, or whatever, and as a result being bullied; even then both the other children and I knew, in an odd way, that I was not going to share their lives in the same kind of detail. Of course the bear, just being the dumb animal that it was, was the 'stranger in the midst', in its most extreme form, that had to be stoned to death.

GF: Moonlight on the Highway *is the story of a disturbed man who escapes from his emotional pain in his obsession with Al Bowlly. We learn that he was sexually assaulted as a child; you yourself have referred to a similarly traumatic incident in your own childhood, in the introduction to* Waiting for the Boat *and in other interviews, which suggests you are again drawing on a personal experience from your own life for the purposes of fiction. As in* Follow the Yellow Brick Road *and* The Singing Detective, *you show the protagonist undergoing psychotherapy in hospital – your attitude to it seems to be one of grudging respect.*

DP: 'Respect' is the right word. 'Grudging' is also the right word because it's an intrusive, rule-bound guessing game that often, by the very irritation of the process, can release enough for the person in therapy to start dealing with. Often it's simply the act of talking to somebody. It was a profession that was practised in the past by others – such as priests. Now it is built into the National Health Service and into the medical fraternity, into social work and agony columns.

Dramatically, it's a very useful device to have someone probing, questioning, seeking to help another adjust to a series of emotional confrontations, and therefore entering into the heart of the turmoil. I use it as a trigger or a shorthand for getting people under stress, who are resisting, to confess or admit or begin to talk about *something* that they wouldn't otherwise articulate, and then to get it out – or some of it. But then they still have to deal with it. I don't say that there's a cure; just that there's a process.

GF: *In those situations where you've shown it, you suggest – rather scathingly – that there's an element of charlatanism in it.*
DP: Oh, there is. But there is in most of those professional or lay contexts. There's the same element of charlatanism at work in architects and lawyers. But there can be the same desire to know the shape of the house you want as there is to be cured of some problem. The very distance between you and the person on the other side of the desk can sometimes formulate what you are wanting to say more swiftly than if you were floundering in your own pool.

GF: Son of Man, *your play about Jesus, is actually one of your most secular plays, I think. You've said that your approach to Jesus was one of 'respectful gnosticism'. Was your main concern a realistic examination of a self-doubting Christ and the politics of those times?*
DP: When I said 'respectful gnosticism', or agnosticism, I think I may have been being slightly dishonest. I must have been aware, and resisting – 'agnosticism' is a badge of resistance, in a way. In terms of Christianity, T. S. Eliot's work shows, in my opinion, that the journey and the doubts and the resistance are more interesting than the arrival, by far. For me, *Son of Man* obviously nods back to the Forest of Dean, the chapel, the strength of those biblical images in my mind, and my assumption that Jesus – the carpenter's son, the Galilean wanderer – was a rebel. It had something to do with my childhood memories, the most vivid ones in terms of literature being from the New Testament and Salem Chapel, that kind of thing. The Forest of Dean is a place where such a wondrous creature would have roamed.

'Agnosticism' is the closest word to what was going on when I wrote that play, but probably a better description of my state would be some kind of yearning, as well as a certain amount of anger at the milk-and-water Christ, the Holman Hunt *Light of the World* Christ, or the Catholic Christ, the supra-mystical, risen-from-the-dead Christ, which is something else – another way of looking at it.

The way it turned out, I was more interested in what Christ did before he preached, what he must have seen as a child in his father's workshop, that sort of Christ. In a way I wanted to strip mysticism away in order to find mysticism – which is a traditional way of doing things.

6 *Son of Man*: Colin Blakeley (centre) as the Galilean rebel

GF: *Does* Son of Man *represent Christ as you believe he may actually have been?*

DP: No, because I have no concept of that. It's a play about *parts* of Christ. When you get a universal hero, whether it's Ulysses or Christ or almost any mythic or near-mythic figure, it's universal simply because so many people can put their own concept and their own culture into it. That even happened with Lenin. There's a human need to universalize an archetypal figure, which is why children love fairy-tales and adults love a different category of fairy-tale. We hunger for archetypal, universaliz-able, mythic or near-mythic figures in order to understand our own dreams and our own mortality.

*Son of Man* was made much worse, in a way, by being shot on video in three days in the electronic studio on a set that looks as though it's trembling and about to fall down, a Galilee that's a sea of glass, the perilous near-fact that you'd see the fourth camera in shot. But it was really a very simple tale, like all those biblical stories – 'Tell me the story, the old, old story, the most wonderful story ever told.' That must have been part of my response to it. But whatever possible strength it might have lurking on the edges is there because I knew I was engaged in that very process. I wrote the play, I delivered it. The BBC came and collected the last pages when I was in hospital in Birmingham. So there was some of that intense physical pressure and pain going on as well – a need for me to say, 'Everything is all right, everything is all right.' Whereas physically, at that time, I don't think it was.

GF: *Were you throwing down a gauntlet to the Church?*

DP: No, I don't believe in throwing down gauntlets, despite appearances to the contrary. Other people have suggested that, including some critics in the past, but I look at them with blank incomprehension because that's not what's in my mind. If I had something to say about the Church I'd write an essay or use a polemic. But I don't think it's a function of drama.

GF: *In the early seventies you embarked on a series of plays that used the motif of a visitor or stranger who's invited indoors, often by a bored or frustrated suburban housewife who has fantasized them into existence. The visitor might be an angel* (Angels Are So Few; Only Make Believe), *a devil* (Brimstone and Treacle), *or a long-lost son* (Schmoedipus) *who stays around long enough to commit an act of liberating violence or sex. Do you regard these plays as religious?*

DP: Only – or maybe a bit more than 'only' – in the sense that drama itself is, and that those patterns of story-telling draw sustenance from that way of looking at human behaviour. The idea of someone who may or may not be outside, but is inside in one sense – i.e. is summoned up as though outside and invited in – is that biblical thing, 'Be not forgetful to entertain strangers: for thereby some have entertained angels unawares' [Hebrews 13:1], or devils or whatever. It's just one of those patterns that needed to be woven.

I find it very difficult to respond to a question like, 'Is that or is that not religious?' or, 'Is that or is that not political?' because I don't know, in that sense. I do know that there are certain structures that recur through fiction and parables and tales and dreams. And one of those is certainly the stranger, the visitor, who either knows more, or comes to punish, or comes to reward – or comes to focus your attention.

GF: *These plays twist the traditional roles played by angels and devils. In the 'Angel Plays' your angels are troubling, disturbed figures, whereas the Devil in* Brimstone *has a positive effect in that his rape of the catatonic girl brings her back to consciousness. In fact you prefaced that play with a quote from Kierkegaard: 'There resides infinitely more good in the demonic man than in the trivial man.'*

DP: Yes. This is where you reach the very edge of what so-called fiction is about. It is very good to be beckoned by old patterns and configurations and structures, but at the same time you've got to subvert them, in order to give them new life. In the case of *Brimstone*, for example, if it had been an angel visiting a troubled house, you wouldn't have had to think at all about it. It would be like one of those coloured religious postcards – it would have been *religiose* instead of religious. Obviously the *type*, the pattern or structure that I was referring to, is that of the guardian angel who visits or protects or spreads wings. A 'visitation', a 'visit', is both a practical description and a metaphor that's deeply coiled up in oral story-telling and religious language. The question therefore becomes: how do you give them flesh and bone? How do you revive the metaphor that has grown stale and become almost second-nature? If you simply turn the coin over and show an angel doing something unexpected then it makes you *see* 'the angel' where otherwise you wouldn't.

As the structuralists say, 'Show how deeply embedded these patterns of thinking are.' They are so deeply embedded they cease to engage the mind, like little aphorisms or clichés or old proverbs that we all understand. One writes a Christmas card without looking at the verse or the picture; whereas if you had a Christmas card in front of you that was

obscene or shocking or utterly astounding you'd think twice before you
signed it, and you'd start to think about Christ, Christmas, images, your
name, your feelings and so on.

That, in shorthand, was what I was trying to do in those plays, by
reversing some of those types: whether it's the angel who is a pathetic
mental patient – it's odd that so many mentally ill people do think of
themselves in those terms – or an extension of the visited person's mind,
or, instead of an angel, the Devil. The fact of new perception, a little
corner being torn in some *canopy* – whether you call it religion or insight
or momentary apprehension of the real truth of a situation – is a dramatic device that freshens, renews, re-examines *why* those images are in
our minds. And yet that perception still serves as a function of those
images. To question something means to *see* it, too, instead of taking it
for granted or dismissing it as an old pattern or cliché. The very act of
readdressing it can sometimes make you see the original pattern more
clearly.

GF: *In* Traitor, *your first play about political treachery, you express
your love of England through romanticism, using Blake and Constable
and Arthur's Camelot as touchstones. The defector Adrian Harris, brilliantly played by John Le Mesurier, movingly laments his lost motherland
in the same way that, at Eton as a boy, he lamented his lost mother. And
yet isn't that a kind of nostalgia for a pastoral England that never really
existed?*
DP: I wasn't just using physical description from paintings or literature –
and after all you can't really call Blake pastoral. I was exploring the long,
deep rhythm of an English native, a rhythm all peoples have, and the
English no less and probably more, than others. In that simple transposition – an Englishman in Russia – what interested me was the mis-
statement that someone could politically betray their country and be
presumed not to love it. The Conservative Party may fly the Union Jack
and play the national anthem and then believe itself to be the patriotic
party, but it's a terrible arrogance to assume what people love about their
culture. Flags and drums and pomp and circumstance are all anathema to
me, whereas there's that long, long, long beat of Englishness which can
be very aggressive but on the whole is slightly melancholy, slightly rueful,
and in many important ways extraordinarily gentle.

That English condition has to do with a collection of things. Obviously
it's basically a human creation, as all culture is. But it's also geographical,
the colour of the sky, the light, the temperature, and the temperamental

island climate; the historical fact that England has not been invaded since 1066; an odd mixture of deference and genuine liberalism; and probably the greatest literature. All of which speak in thousands of voices. Add the fact that everyone loves his or her native patch, sometimes dangerously so. Strip away things like nationalism and militarism and Empire, and those flags and drums and trumpets and so on, and you're still left with a considerable body of *something* to which, not uncritically, God forbid, you emotionally respond, in the same way as you acknowledge your own parents.

GF: *Is betrayal of one's country morally acceptable if the end justifies the means? Philby, Burgess, Maclean and Blunt were products of the communist ferment at Cambridge in the thirties and believed, arguably, in a greater good than English patriotism.*

DP: I thought they were detestable people. But it's partly because I detested them so much that I wanted to find some saving grace in them, and I tried to show that in *Traitor*. I did that also in *Blade on the Feather*, where the quivering don, Cavendish, when faced with a gun, tries to define the roots of his betrayal. He says that all spies, without exception, are upper-class: 'I was born into a class that loves what it owns. And we don't own quite enough of it any more, that is why all, all, not just some but all of the renowned traitors working for Nazi Germany or Stalin's Russia, all come from my class.' There is that patrician element in the English upper classes which makes them willing to sell out anything to anybody at any time. Even though they appear to foreigners to be the ultra-English, they are – to me anyway – the *least* English-like of all the English.

GF: *Frankly, the way you have written them, neither Adrian Harris in* Traitor *nor Jason Cavendish in* Blade on the Feather *emerges as detestable.*

DP: No, I hope not. But that was my starting point. That's what I feel politically about them. Knowing that, I then felt I wanted to find out how they could have justified themselves – beyond reading Stalin. Even if they had the excuse, or the partial excuse, of saying, 'We didn't know what the consequences would be,' it's a bit like saying to the Nazis, 'What do you mean you didn't know about what was happening to the Jews?' In the end theirs was not a tenable position, in any shape or form. And to occupy that untenable position must have taken not only an arrogance about their own intellect and social position, but also a love of power, of

7    *Traitor*: John Le Mesurier, Jack Headley
8    *Blade on the Feather*: 'visitor' Daniel Young (Tom Conti)
and traitor Jason Cavendish (Donald Pleasence)

being on the winning side, as well as any motivation toward social justice, toward communism in its ideal form, some complicated mix of idealism and guilt.

GF: *The betrayal of Cavendish by the visitor – the Tom Conti character – at the end of* Blade on the Feather *could be described as reactionary.*
DP: Sure, because the Conti character is a Soviet spy and Soviet spies were reactionary. Both these men are the antithesis of what I take to be the essential Englishman – who is non-ideological, slightly philistine, genuinely liberal, mostly tolerant, complacent, pragmatic, competent in many wrong ways, but much, much more interesting than those who commit themselves to an ideology. Orwell was somebody who understood this.

GF: *Were these characters, Adrian Harris in* Traitor *and Cavendish in* Blade on the Feather, *amalgams of Philby, Burgess, Maclean and Blunt, or an impression of them filtered through your own imagination?*
DP: I hope the latter. You get a starting point from what people talk about or from the newspapers, but they become, one hopes, people. They're not there in order to illustrate anything, and although they *may* illustrate something, that's not *why* they are there. You want to know them as people.

GF: *Adrian Harris seems to be closer to Kim Philby than to anybody else. Why not just take Philby?*
DP: Because it's less interesting, and because he's known, and people would say, 'Oh, *Kim Philby.*' That would be a ready-made package, even though it's likely to be as fictive as the one you're dealing with. Because of the area you're in you want to give a nod to what people know about or think they know about someone like Philby. But to make it directly Philby would be to enter a sphere of writing that I am just simply, matter-of-factly, finally and emphatically, not interested in.

GF: *Do you think the same impulses that draw you to write about political betrayal are the same impulses that draw you to write about other kinds of betrayal, particularly sexual betrayal?*
DP: I don't know. Betrayal is betrayal is betrayal. The dictionary definition of the word has the same meaning for all kinds.

GF: *It's more pronounced in your work than perhaps in those other writers working consistently over the same period. It's there over and over again. From Nigel Barton's betrayal of his classmate, to the uncle's betrayal of his niece by stealing her life for his novel in* Blackeyes, *and so on.*

DP: Maybe there's something I don't know or want to know. But betrayal is the long receding prism of human life. It's the *truth* about us. Our first allegiances cannot be sustained.

GF: *Our first allegiance is to our mother, probably.*

DP: That can't be sustained either. Our first allegiances are based upon Eden. The whole story of human culture is based upon the original sin. It's an inescapable fact of our mortality. When we're young we feel 'the bright shoots of everlastingness' but later we laugh at that, and we laugh tenderly. We laugh with a mixture of awe and regret, because we know it cannot be sustained. But if we lose it altogether then we lose something essential, we lose the bud in the flower, we lose the possibilities of regeneration.

It's the gap between the first perceptions of perfection and our later selves that tries us. But how wide the gap is what counts. There is going to be a gap – how do you measure it? If you feel merely nostalgia and contempt, and respond with a satirical twist of the face, if you simply *mock*, then something has been killed inside you. If you feel remorse, regret, guilt . . . well, that's better, but something has still been killed. If you feel a tension between the wish to preserve some of whatever idealism, whatever faith, whatever 'purity' you first perceived, and a rueful acknowledgement that a journey has been made away from that, and yet can still preserve *some* of it, and more and more maybe, then that's human.

GF: *Is that why, to put it simplistically, many of your plays have supposedly happy endings, or at least offer a gesture of hope?*

DP: Do they? I have no idea whether that's true or not.

GF: *Is it something you don't particularly want to address?*

DP: No. I simply have no idea whether that is the case or not. Each piece has its own grammar or its own shape.

GF: *The protagonists in* Follow the Yellow Brick Road *and* Double Dare, *as well as in all three of your novels, are their own authorial deities – yet they are not really in control of their own lives.*

DP: They are and they aren't. Even saying to yourself, 'I'm not in control,' is a way of being in control, to a degree. It's a way of dealing with being out of control. If there's a very strong wind blowing and you're walking across the moor, no matter what you do, say or think, you can't quite walk upright; if it rains, you get wet. In that sense we're not in control. We're going to age, we're going to die – all those things. Or somebody's going to give you the sack. It can be quite random, like Jesus saying, 'Rain falls on the just and the unjust.' But what sort of argument is that?

GF: *In* Follow the Yellow Brick Road – *which you once described as a religious play – you've got a manic-depressive commercials actor imagining he's being followed around by a television camera. What did that signify to you?*

DP: It's a metaphor for a kind of paranoia, where he imagines every little thing as well as every big thing he does is being observed, and that the evidence is being used in a plot against him. In a way he has the reverse side of the desire that everything should be pure. And to him the only pure things – because they had no subversive messages, they were just selling things – were those happy families, those sunlit fields, those blue skies and those wondrous jingles of the commercials. Because he was a failed actor and the only parts he could appear to get were in those little mini-dramas – the happy, happy, happy commercials – and because life is incapable of that, he felt that life was soiled. All the grace and joy which religious people can sometimes feel was translated by him into the commercials, as opposed to the 'filthy' drama, the 'filthy' plays, the 'filthy' films, the way people appear to *sneak* in the social life around him. Because he was ill the commercials became the only touchstone by which he could judge the degree of degradation around him.

This is why the play ends with the double irony of a voice-over – for a commercial for pills – in which he quotes the Epistle to the Philippians: 'Whatsoever things are true, whatsoever things are honest, whatsoever things are just, whatsoever things are lovely, whatsoever things are of good report' and so on. You see him doing this in the television studio. It becomes a parody, a satire, a bitter comment on the way religious people can drip honey and sugar upon everything, even an earthquake or a terrible human mutilation. They'll say 'God understands' or something.

GF: *In* Only Make Believe, *you show a physically and emotionally disabled writer dictating a play to an unresponsive typist, with whom he's desperately trying to connect. The play he is dictating is your own* Angels

Are So Few, *which went on the air three years earlier. What's the specific relationship between the two plays – are they dependent on one another?*
DP: My memory is that they were meant to be part of a trilogy, conceived under the generic title of *Visitors*. God knows what happened to the third one. It probably didn't get written, or was abandoned, or was interfered with. It was just contingency that the script the writer was dictating in *Only Make Believe* was *Angels Are So Few*. Of course I'm always suspicious when people say that – as the Marxists say, there's no such thing as coincidence. But I wouldn't have thought there was much of a relationship between those plays, except they're both about damage: sexual inhibition and deep sexual anxiety.

GF: *At the end of* Joe's Ark, *the pet-shop proprietor, Joe, is reunited with his estranged son after his daughter has died of cancer, and once again a visitor – in this case a self-centred student – is the agent of renewal. It shares with* Brimstone *the need to find, to paraphrase Cardinal Hume, 'some God in the cancer', and, like* Brimstone, *ends on an optimistic note.*
DP: Well, maybe.

GF: *Was it your battles with your own illness that prompted these plays?*
DP: Who knows? There are some things that it is inevitable I should use. Since the dominant facts of my life are pressing against my eyeballs or my mind a lot of the time it's inevitable that they should creep, or actually march sometimes, into the things I am writing about. But to *re*-rephrase the Cardinal, I am as interested in finding 'the cancer in God'.

GF: *That becomes clear in Joe's renunciation of the chapel.*
DP: It's not like Thomas Hardy shaking his fist against what he called 'the President of the Immortals'. It's simply that ordinary human feeling of being abandoned and betrayed and left to endure. Even if a tree struck by lightning falls across a car, killing a little girl in the back seat, you can't say, 'God is working His purpose out.' You can't bellow one of those hymns and understand why a cat tortures a mouse.

GF: *I want to push you on this question of optimism. You could have left Joe entirely bereft in his pet-shop with the rain pouring down. You needn't have brought him and his son together.*
DP: But I don't know whether that's the cancer or the God, do I? That's one of the knots that was left untied. The brother's despair was as great as his sister's, although she was a better person than he was, with his

desperation, his filthy jokes and his miserable act on the pub circuit – nothing *means* nothing with him. I know there had obviously been a bond between them by some of the asides in her dialogue. It's possible to imagine they had a very close relationship. And there's the fact, as every-one knows from their own circumstances, that during a crisis everything is momentarily refocused. The father and the brother needed, for their own different reasons – and they might have been wrong – to see some significance in the fact of her young death. Otherwise they couldn't even begin to come to terms with it. But maybe, whether they could or could not come to terms with it, there is significance in it anyway.

A preacher would say, 'Yes, there is significance.' An atheist would say, 'No, that is simply a human lie; it has no meaning at all. There's just oblivion and you have to accept it – that's the way things are.' I could have written the play from either angle. In my opinion, though, it would have been less interesting written from either angle – somewhere in the tension between the possibilities is where drama lives, without one saying, 'Oh, it meant this and it meant that.' It can mean 'this' *and* 'that' at the same time.

GF: *So you proceed from an unregimented position?*
DP: It's regimented when a writer has very strong opinions about these things, and *imposes* those opinions upon what it is they're writing. I don't believe I do that – I hope I don't.

GF: *Does the ambivalence in your work mean you're leaving it up to the viewer to make up his or her mind?*
DP: I don't give a fuck what the viewer thinks, to be honest. If there's something there for you to inject thoughts into or superimpose feelings on to, to understand or misunderstand, that's fine – but that's always the case with fiction. When fiction ceases to be fiction it's when the author is driving toward a little slot or pocket where it can *only* go. When that happens, in my opinion, it's not fiction. It ceases to be metaphorical, it ceases to have resonances – it becomes an argument, which is a very legitimate form of literature belonging to prose and the essay and the polemic. It does not belong to drama.

GF: *Is this something you have determined for yourself or is it simply that you prefer to be non-dogmatic?*
DP: It's just something that happens when you're writing. You might start out with conceptions of what the argument (using 'argument'

loosely) is. If you maintain it in the face of your own evidence, what these characters feel and do, then it becomes something else. Then you should abandon it, and write the argument in some other form. The only thing that has inherited both the older, parable form of religion and the possibilities of discourse not being cast in argument form is drama. Not even the novel can do it.

GF: *In* Only Make Believe, *and also in* Double Dare *and* The Singing Detective, *you show writers in the grip of the struggle to write. And if, as you say, these works aren't autobiographical, I assume that they must at least be deeply personal because you're showing the anxieties of being an author.*

DP: Or simply that it is hard to write.

GF: *Are you using the writer's condition as a window into universal experience?*

DP: I hope not. It's very dangerous if I am. I use writers probably because I've run out of knowledge about what other people do for a living. And there is that one remote sense in which trying to describe anything becomes a journey. It has that in common with most people's jobs, to a degree. Writing, the reclusiveness that goes with it, in my case health problems, is what I most vividly and practically and most intensely know. It's that that's my work, and that's what I have sometimes used.

I guess at those writers' struggles. I don't – maybe alas! – have many of those blocks or difficulties. I just get on with it. But it does occur to me, as I facilely cover the pages, what it would be like not to be able to write – which is probably the source of some of those alleged 'sufferings' the writers have in my plays.

GF: *Have you ever suffered from writer's block?*

DP: Once or twice maybe, and then I melodramatized it into something else. In other words, even while it was a so-called block I knew it wasn't really.

GF: *It was a means to an end perhaps?*

DP: It was a means to draw something else out of myself, yes.

GF: *In* Brimstone and Treacle, *the visitor, Martin, literally plays devil's advocate when he leads the reactionary Mr Bates into confronting the idea of concentration camps for West Indian immigrants in England, an idea which Mr Bates rejects. Because Martin is perhaps a figment of Mr Bates's and his wife's imaginations, were you therefore showing how a decent but disappointed middle-class Englishman might rationalize ideas of good and evil to himself?*

DP: I think it was much more down-to-earth than that. Although the consequences of many things people think about can be extraordinarily evil, I don't think they acknowledge that. And I think if it's put directly to them – not in terms of hectoring them and saying, 'You're scum', but in terms of a sympathetic extension into logic of what they actually do think – people recoil from what they *think* they think. In this case the father of a very sick daughter has a picture of his culture or his country or his position that is more than half true, but not sufficiently true. And out of that, triggered by immense disappointment on all levels – by his job, his wife, obviously by his damaged daughter, but also by his own sexuality – he extended the dream of what life *could* be like, and blamed its failure upon the visitors, the immigrants, the fact that an old lady couldn't 'feel safe on the streets at night' – which is true in some parts. And in his ideal world he wishes that they'd never come. But when he realizes that they *are* here, that the great majority were *born* here, and that the only way of enforcing their departure is by raids in the night, by gathering them up into a concentration camp system and inflicting barbarism on them, the more troubled he becomes. The simple image he had of what England was like before, and what it could be like if changes hadn't happened, couldn't take in the fact of change, nor the results of trying to reverse change. And I believe people are like that – but only a few of them, those who are utterly mad and sick. Sometimes they have more energy than the rest of us and actually gain political power, but only in times of crisis.

GF: *Not that it makes him any less culpable, but Mr Bates's racism is founded on received ideas.*

DP: He was also ashamed of belonging to the National Front; he didn't want anyone to know. In the mid-seventies, when I wrote that play, the National Front vote had gone up to 10 or 12 per cent in some constituencies; it looked threatening. The things he says, though, are just shouts, like all extreme right- or left-wing ideas, across an imagined, mythic barricade, behind which is perfection, and in front of which is total evil.

GF: *Do you think the mother's little thread of Christian faith is actually the restorative power in this play?*

DP: I wouldn't go so far as that, but she is the only one whose wishes come true. Even though she is the mocked one, the scorned one, and even though she's stupid and simple and easily manipulated, she is the only one who actually believes in the visitor.

GF: *It's that belief that triggers the miracle, no matter how violently it is achieved.*

DP: You could say that. But it's not *like* that, either in life or in that particular little play. Some of it is accidental, contingent. Some of it is coincidence in the old sense of the word. She is the only one whose prayer is answered that way. That's sufficient. That's all you need to know.

GF: *It's not part of a master plan?*

DP: There are no master plans.

GF: *Do you remember how you reacted when* Brimstone and Treacle *was banned?*

DP: I wasn't too pleased. It was made and it was due to go out; it was listed in the *Radio Times* for that week. If it was going to be stopped it should have been either at the script stage or in the production stage or in the editing stage or in the delivery of the final show. But it was none of those things. It was as if someone had made a very late trawl through the week's viewing and said to the powers that be, 'You'd better see this.' There's not much more I can say about that. I understood Alasdair Milne. I understand *better* now. He just found it repellent.

GF: *'Diabolical' – and it's a wonderful irony – is the word he used to describe the play.*

DP: 'Diabolical' is a very good word. It's amazing how often people inadvertently use as a term of abuse something which accurately portrays what is going on. It *was* diabolical, but not of course in the sense that he meant.

GF: *Your play* Where Adam Stood *was inspired by Edmund Gosse's* Father and Son *(1907), which is regarded as one of the great autobiographies.*

DP: It is. I'm not entirely sure it's a truthful one, but it's beautifully written. I only took a few pages of it. The play is in no sense an adaptation.

GF: *You focus on the emotional struggle between the young Gosse and*

9   *Where Adam Stood*: the father (Alan Badel)
10  *Where Adam Stood*: the son (Max Harris)

*his widowed father, a naturalist and fundamentalist Christian preacher,*
*and on the father's philosophical struggle with the Darwinists. Did that*
*clash between Darwinism and Christianity speak directly to you?*
DP: No, but I did feel great sympathy for intelligent fundamentalists
who had clearly, in some senses, deluded themselves into saying that the
Bible, and the Book of Genesis in particular, is literally true. I'm not
talking about ignorant, prating fundamentalists – I'm talking about
people like Philip Gosse, the father, and many others, who were deeply
shaken by Darwin's theories, as was Darwin himself. Not that Darwin
was a fundamentalist, but he was aware of the consequences. What
interested me was that Sir Charles Lyell and a few other geologists and
naturalists were already indicating that Darwin was right, but Philip
Gosse used all his considerable intellect to write his own explanation,
which in its own way has a certain beauty and grace. He wrote a book
called *Omphalos*, which is Greek for 'navel', and he explained that
although Adam had a belly-button he had no mother. And this led Gosse
to a wonderful sequence where he explains why this should be by saying
God wanted Adam to be the model of what human beings would be like.
Therefore he had to have a belly-button – which implies an umbilical
cord, which implies a mother! Moreover, when Adam looked around
he'd see that the hills were already old, and as part of that there would
have been fossils in those hills. Do you see how complicated it gets in
terms of being able to maintain what was thought to be important literal
belief in Genesis, but which he knew as a scientist to be disproved by
incontrovertible evidence to the contrary? That's what interests me about
faith – that it can try and join up those two things. But what Gosse was
doing was recommending, in terms of one discourse, *another* discourse,
and you can never do that – a spade's a spade. What he was attempting
was something that is closer to poetry. It has nothing to do with literal
truth, but he thought it did and he suffered in consequence.

GF: *When Edmund tells his father that God said he could have the*
*model sailing ship in the shop window, is he deliberately using the same*
*kind of logic as the father has in convincing himself that Genesis is true?*
DP: The little boy, whose mother has just died, has been watching all
this and having to endure it. When the father says to the child, 'Why
don't you ask God if you can have the sailing ship?' he thinks his power
is so great that the child will obediently say God told him he couldn't
have it. But the father has got mixed up over what is God, what is habit
and what is parental authority, and the boy's first act of rebellion is deep

within the father's religious language. When the child says God says he can have the ship, the father can't deny it, because the boy has observedly prayed. The same thing had happened to the father. It shows how one language does not relate to another. The shape of the little drama is exactly like the Garden of Eden, and the boy's final self-knowledge is like Adam and Eve's self-knowledge. It's the boy who draws the line, it's the boy who stops his father coming into his room to talk by putting a chair against the door. It's probably the most complicated and probably the best of all the things, in that sense, that I've tried to do. It's the most complete statement of all those difficulties that yet remain very simple.

GF: *Does the madwoman's sexual attack on Edmund somehow precipitate the ending, too? Is it showing the word made flesh?*

DP: It was just one of those things that would happen in a village at that time, one of the realizations that the world is different and more complicated than the simple vision God is giving you. I am feeling uncomfortable. Please move on.

GF: *The villagers' stoning of the bear in* A Beast with Two Backs *was echoed in the boys killing the squirrel in* Blue Remembered Hills. *That cruelty, and the way people round upon the weakest among them, stresses that in childhood exist all of the behavioural patterns of the adult. It's amplified most fully in your use of grown-ups playing children in* Stand Up, Nigel Barton *and* Blue Remembered Hills, *what you've described as 'the magnifying glass of the adult body'.*

DP: I was trying to avoid twee and coy responses – 'Ah, look at those children.' If you are seven and the bully is seven, then it's as bad, as terrifying, as being mugged on the street as an adult. If you saw two child actors doing it it could still be terrifying, but there is something that distances you from it, and you say, 'That is what children are like.' Whereas if it's two adults it's so close to what adults actually *do* do. You just add the fidgets and the constant movement of children.

   *Blue Remembered Hills* was the first time that I couldn't allow myself long speeches – because children don't speak that way – or consecutive thought, in the A-B-C-D-E sense, because children don't think that way. The constant switches of their attention meant that it was the most straightforward, the most apparently naturalistic play I'd done – except that it was played by *adults*.

   The odd thing was that the first few minutes of it were terrifying for me because I wondered if it was going to work! When Colin Welland comes charging out of that field, splashing into a puddle, making aeroplane noises and crashing, it could have been the most embarrassing thing ever. I think most audiences start thinking of the characters as children about five minutes into it. And yet at the same time you're looking at adults, and you *know* you're looking at adults, so you see the double bounce. Why do people often say, 'I dreamt I was back in school'? It's a version of a nightmare – a recurring one for some people, though not for me, thank God. But I have often heard it said, and I have often read that people frequently, when anxious, dream of their schooldays, of their teacher's question, to which they don't know the answer . . .

So there is such a balance in our own selves. Obviously the child is father to the man, and obviously we carry our childhoods within us. That goes without saying. But to see those little hierarchies, that competitiveness, those casual brutalities physically dramatized by adult bodies, that was what I was after – and the sudden tendernesses: they cry about the squirrel they've stoned to death, or at least one of them starts crying and the others get embarrassed and they start shuffling about. They deal with their emotions in a very English way, by turning upon the one who causes them discomfort. But the other thing, of course, is that the English are very skilled at repressing emotion, which children aren't, not in quite the same way, and certainly not primary school children. You've just got to look at a playground.

So a lot of those things were going on in *Blue Remembered Hills* and in *Stand Up, Nigel Barton*, when Nigel is called to the front and made to read from the Bible, and suddenly realizes the meaning of what he is reading, having, as it were, plunged somebody into trouble. I virtually duplicated the scene in *The Singing Detective*, quite deliberately, so that when Marlow is talking to the therapist it presages his trying to stand up. He's made to encounter that casual betrayal from all those years before, the kind of betrayal or cruelty or deceit, whatever it is, that each one of us has committed. It's very valuable in life, in knowing the shape of your own life, when you know that some part of your childhood has thrown up some memory or some casual thing that has recurred decade upon decades later. It's very valuable dramatically, and it's a truism of psycho-analysis. It's true when you look at family albums – you can see there as a child the person that you are now.

GF: *I was going to suggest that you used the A. E. Housman lines, which you read yourself at the end of* Blue Remembered Hills, *ironically – but then I'm not so sure that you did.*

11    *Blue Remembered Hills*: Colin Jeavons, Michael Elphick,
Janine Duvitski, Colin Welland, Robin Ellis, John Bird,
and Helen Mirren

DP: No, I don't think there was much irony there. There's always a tinge of it, alas. It says in the most simple way, 'Where have they gone, those blue remembered hills?' There's an irony about the 'land of lost content', because there is no such land, never can be. And yet there's a yearning to be able to go back and put things right. There is irony in terms of the story, and yet the yearning within that little poem is *non*-ironic. Just as I was using the adult body for the child's, so I'm using genuine yearning ironically, but without the irony being the point. It's the same kind of double-focus going on.

GF: *After* Blue Remembered Hills *you decamped to LWT. Did you break from the BBC at this time because of the* Brimstone *banning and because they had made you buy back the rights of* Pennies from Heaven?
DP: They were factors in it. A certain natural degree of 'Up yours!' was going on. But it was also understanding the way things were starting to go in television, and of course they've gone much further since. It was a realization that you couldn't put every single egg in a basket that might not hold them. There were big holes already in the basket, and your egg might have been smaller than you thought!

GF: *You originally had six plays scheduled at LWT, but only three of them –* Blade on the Feather, Rain on the Roof *and* Cream in my Coffee *– ended up getting made. Have any of the others resurfaced?*
DP: No. One of them was about Hitler in the Bunker in 1945 and the fact that there were children there, Goebbels's children.

GF: *Was it to be seen through the children's eyes?*
DP: I'm not entirely sure now. Half and half, I suspect. They were little blond kids, about five of them, and their great joy, apparently, was to sing to Uncle Adolf. They all knew the game was up and yet fantasy had also taken over. Also, there was this whole thing about Hitler being a vegetarian. It seemed to me that in such a nightmarish scenario there must be something to say about all of us. Maybe it's just as well I didn't try to write it. I'm still tempted, though.

GF: *Each of the three LWT plays was shot on film. Did that require any change in visual grammar for you, or did you tailor the scripts for film?*
DP: Not specifically, but I must have been partly aware of that. I must have allowed myself to jump somewhere that I wouldn't normally have

done. I find that difficult to answer because I don't even know whether I've attended to it or not.

GF: Rain on the Roof *is another visitation play with an Oedipal theme. A young wife, whose husband has been cheating on her, flirts with the illiterate youth she's teaching to read and he eventually kills the husband, or so it seems. But it's primarily a play about words and language – the couple are called 'Janet and John', the husband's a copywriter.*

DP: It's also about condescension. The woman is giving the boy a great gift when she says, 'I will teach you to read,' but somehow it's got tangled up in a very English way with her feeling, 'I am better than you are,' and 'How good of me to do this for you.' Because that is the mechanism of how she teaches him to read as an adult, some older rebellion breaks out in him. All the shame and tension and violence he feels in not being able to read turns him against the angel who's teaching him. Teaching is a very delicate and dangerous relationship, isn't it? That's why parenthood is so difficult.

The play is about the power of words, but it's more importantly about power between these sorts of people. The teacher is more powerful. She is also female. She also has the key to all these words and what they may or may not mean.

There was an early echo of that in *Where the Buffalo Roam*, where the young man's path to literacy was blocked. Because he was interested in the Western, that might have been the path, but it seems he didn't want it to be. But there was nobody communicating with him. A probation officer was trying to, but as soon as that relationship got slightly off-key it actually triggered the violence. Similarly with *Rain on the Roof*.

GF: *Was the casting of Cheryl Campbell in* Rain on the Roof *made obvious by her having played the schoolteacher in* Pennies from Heaven?

DP: I don't know about 'obvious', but I certainly said to the director, Alan Bridges, 'God, she'd play this part well.' The evidence of what she could do was right in front of us. So why not? For some things there are part-explanations, and for others accidental explanations. Nobody moves in a totally abstract way in these things. There are too many symmetries sought after the event which you can't really plan for in advance: if you do a certain thing they will be there whether you know it or not. Whether *I* know it or not they will be there.

GF: *In the third of the LWT plays,* Cream in my Coffee, *you addressed*

*the notion of 'personal sovereignty', to use your own phrase, and what*
*can happen to a person if they are unable to gather up 'the shreds of their*
*sovereign selves'. A well-to-do young man, Bernard, runs off with his*
*fiancée, Jean, for a dirty weekend at a South Coast hotel, and then –*
*summoned home by his domineering mother – leaves her there to be*
*seduced by the hotel's dance-band singer. Forty years later they return to*
*the hotel, where we see that Bernard's class-driven condescension to Jean*
*has turned into cruelty. His embitterment seems to be the consequence of*
*his earlier weakness.*

DP: It's about those dances between what was and what is. To fall in
love, to fall into an emotional and sexual relationship, and at the same
time to know that those feelings will end, is enormously difficult – in a
sense, impossible. But if you write about it you see that that long, ten-
league boot stride is what happens to what was allegedly so ardently felt.
When the couple in *Cream* return, years later, to the very place where in
the past you would have seen him declaring his love to her, the husband
almost within seconds has become tetchy and bad-tempered. He's resisting the pull of the past. It's perilously close to cynicism, but it isn't,
because it shows what we do, what we *have* to do, to retain anything like
the substance of what we were; those feelings were *once* authentic. That's
what drama does. I've seen it done in novels, but it would take you
several hundred pages. In drama you can juxtapose the past and the
present in a way that doesn't *tell*, but *shows*.

GF: *But we have an incurable faith in the possibility of love surviving,*
*and the need to embark on that journey, even when we know it's going to*
*end.*
DP: We know it's going to be different – so how authentic, therefore, are
those declarations? If they really are authentic then you do everything in
your power to retain what they meant.

GF: *Jean sexually betrays Bernard in* Cream in my Coffee. *And even if he*
*deserves to be betrayed, we could be forgiven for pointing a moralistic*
*finger at her.*
DP: I know. But she, interestingly, is the kindly one later on in their lives.
She is the one who is cosseting and caring, even though abused by the old
man. You can see the old man in the young man, I hope. You can see
enough signs that he shouldn't be behaving as he does: in his slight
about-face, his potential petulance, and his cowardice, too, in not standing up to his mother.

12   *Cream in my Coffee*: Bernard and Jean (Peter Chelsom and
Shelagh McLeod)

13   *Cream in my Coffee*: Bernard and Jean – forty years later (Peggy
Ashcroft and Lionel Jeffries)

14 *Cream in my Coffee*: Martin Shaw as the predatory singer of cheap songs

GF: *Allowing her to be seduced by the dance-band singer – the predatory singer of cheap songs – is like an act of wilful self-castration.*

DP: Yes. He clothes her in old songs, but they are sung by someone else. And years later he forgets the tune.

# CHAPTER 3

# In Other Writers' Heads

*Casanova, Late Call, The Mayor of Casterbridge,*
*Tender is the Night, Christabel*

'Novelty is the tyrant of my soul.'
Casanova in *Casanova*

'I do not think that other people's worlds suit Potter,' wrote Peter Lennon in his review of *Christabel* for the *Listener* in 1988. 'He is surprisingly subdued by them.' Television dramatist Alan Plater, in the same journal, the same year, 'It could be argued . . . that the world's leading authorities on *Tender is the Night* and *Bleak House* are Dennis Potter and Arthur Hopcraft: a proposition to send many a flutter through the Sacred Groves of Academe . . . [But] Potter will always be more dangerous than Fitzgerald/Potter.'

With the exception of *Casanova* (1971) the serials Potter has based on the work of other writers are not generally recalled with the same affection or critical esteem as *Pennies from Heaven* and *The Singing Detective* (and certainly not with the anger that greeted *Blackeyes*). This may partly be explained by the force of Potter's non-naturalistic methods, the 'surprise element' that audiences have come to expect from him since the time of *Pennies* and *Blue Remembered Hills*, and which are largely absent in *The Mayor of Casterbridge* (1978), *Tender is the Night* (1985) and *Christabel*. Out of respect for the authors of those books, or more reliably the belief that his own techniques might betray their inner life, he has kept their narratives essentially linear and third-person. To neglect them on this score, however, is to underestimate their power as adaptations that render the true spirit of their sources – underpinned in each case by a hidden psychology that the authors themselves might not have been aware of, but which Potter certainly is.

The most obvious example of this is *Tender is the Night*, based by Potter on F. Scott Fitzgerald's second version of his novel, published in 1934, about the tragic French Riviera love story of psychiatrist Dick Diver (Peter Strauss) and his wife and patient Nicole Warren (Mary Steenburgen). 'I was drawn to the book by the odd sort of sheen on

Fitzgerald's prose, which has never in my opinion been caught,' Potter said in an interview.* 'There's something which is not in the dialogue, which is not even in the characters – it's in that fable element. The book is partly about Americans in Europe, partly about Fitzgerald and Zelda, it's partly about his unease and fear of what is going to happen to him, it's about exile, and it's a fable done in a realistic manner. And the fable of this doomed couple is in direct contradiction to the American experience of popular art.'

*Casanova*, Potter's first serial for television, a six-parter written over a period of thirteen months, was inspired by Giacomo Casanova's posthumously published twelve-volume *Mémoires* (1826–38), rather than 'adapted' from it, and is as personal and powerful a work of imagination as Potter's original serials. Potter has described Casanova's writing as 'vain and egotistical', but he saw in his amorous triumphs the seeds of conflict and a theme that particularly suited the era of free love and Mary Whitehouse. Much less a classic costume drama than a modernist deconstruction of the Casanova myth, Potter's drama – featuring a brilliant and sympathetic performance by Frank Finlay as a tormented aesthete – depicts a man entrapped as much by his libido as by the religious mores of the eighteenth century which have literally entrapped him in a prison cell (a five-year sentence for 'foul atheism'). As he lies rotting in jail, Casanova's mind whirls back and forth between the agonies of his incarcerated present and often melancholy recollections of his libertine past as he gropes toward final redemption. The metaphor of the prison cell, the preoccupation with memory ('Sounds, smells, carry us back . . . like ravening wolves of the past . . . bouncing one memory against another'), the doubling of actor Norman Rossington as both Casanova's jailer and an English traveller, are among the Potteresque tropes of a serial which, as both chamber-piece and identity quest, strongly anticipated *The Singing Detective*.

Potter's 1975 dramatization of Angus Wilson's 1964 novel *Late Call* is the story of a woman hotelier, Sylvia Calvert (Dandy Nichols), who retires with her husband, a feckless old soldier, to the new-town home of their widowed headmaster son and his three children. A neglected work in Potter's canon, it is a quietly authoritative, mainly straightforward explication of the generational conflicts, rooted in the son's repressed anguish at his wife's death and the problems the old couple has in adjusting to the overbearingly middle-class community. In one crucial respect,

---

* From 'Dennis in Wonderland', interview with James Saynor, *Stills*, November 1985.

however, the play diverges from linear narrative, in showing Sylvia's recurrent memory of a day from her childhood when, as the daughter of a serving woman, she and an upper-class charge had taken their petticoats off and splashed in a stream. The threat of punishment for the incident resounds in Sylvia's mind during the present-day upheaval, enigmatically informing her need to embolden herself in her new surroundings. The return of the repressed is an integral theme in Potter's work.

Potter's seven-part *The Mayor of Casterbridge* was part of the halcyon era of 'classical' serials that were made under the stewardship of the late Martin Lisemore (producer of *Our Mutual Friend* and *I, Claudius*) and Jonathan Powell at the BBC in the late seventies. As well as *Casterbridge*, Powell produced *Crime and Punishment, Pride and Prejudice* and *Thérèse Raquin*, and he would later oversee *Tender is the Night*. Potter had previously contributed *A Tragedy of Two Ambitions* to the BBC 2 *Wessex Tales* anthology of Hardy stories; given his upbringing in the Forest of Dean, which lies north-west of 'Wessex', just across the Severn, he was an obvious choice to write the corporation's ambitious drama of the Thomas Hardy novel, which was originally published in serial form itself and which Robert Louis Stevenson had wanted to see dramatized. The tragedy of a hay-trusser, Michael Henchard (Alan Bates), who sells his wife and daughter at a village fair then rises to merchant and mayor and is eventually destroyed by his early mistake, was treated with absolute fidelity by Potter. Not least of the serial's achievements is its characterization of Henchard as a repressed man in the grip of the 'malignity of fate' and his own psychological weaknesses. The opening sequence, when he drunkenly auctions Susan (Anne Stallybrass) and the young Elizabeth-Jane (Janet Maw), is a remarkable dramatic transposition of one of the most chilling first chapters in literature.

Originally conceived as a movie by Potter, *Christabel* was dramatized in four parts from Christabel Bielenberg's 1968 memoir *The Past is Myself*, about her life as an Englishwoman in Nazi Germany. The title of the book alone must have intrigued Potter, who optioned it after reading a review of it in *The Economist* in 1983, although he says he was attracted to it by its housewifely, humanistic perceptions of the war. In 1934 Christabel Burton, a well-to-do niece of Lord Northcliffe, had married the German, Oxford-educated liberal law student Peter Bielenberg and moved with him to Hamburg, where they had two sons. In 1944 Bielenberg was implicated in the 20 July plot to assassinate Hitler, and imprisoned in the Ravensbrück concentration camp, where Christabel visited him. She saw out the war in the Black Forest and was reunited with her husband in 1945. They now live in Ireland.

Except for a sequence in which Christabel (Elizabeth Hurley) dreams of her Blimpish father being bayoneted by Nazi paratroopers in his stately home, while Peter (Stephen Dillon), in Gestapo black, takes aim at his blushing bride, *Christabel* is naturalistic and linear, although over-laid with a fairy-tale veneer. Potter's plays and films frequently quote Lewis Carroll, and here he sends his plummy-voiced Alice up against the Anschluss and the Holocaust and down among the ruins of Berlin as her countrymen pulverize it from above. Hitler is evoked as a 'malignant hobgoblin' and the story culminates in a Grimm Black Forest village (echoing the Forest of Dean) with a family reunion purloined from *The Sound of Music*. Until that sentimental finale, *Christabel* is a restrained soap opera that uses the very banality of its central romance and its domestic scenes as a window on to the bigger picture of the war, and which traces its young heroine's slow-burning politicization. Most effec-tive is the way Potter avoids genre expectations by shearing off the aggressively Allied perspective of the Second World War mini-series and allowing everything German to seem 'English': when Christabel returns to Berlin after visiting Peter and hides out in the firestorm with an old lady (played by 'Cockney' actress Edna Doré, of *EastEnders* and *High Hopes*), it is the London Blitz which is empathetically evoked.

GF: *In* Late Call, *which you adapted from the Angus Wilson novel, you show an old woman, unsettled by having moved to an unfamiliar environment, recalling an incident from her adolescence and the first inchoate stirrings of her sexuality. She remembers being chastised for taking her petticoat off and splashing in a country stream on a hot summer morning in 1911. What inspired you here?*

DP: Sometimes people approach you to do something and it can be as much a stimulus as what generally holds your interest. The BBC asked me to do *Late Call*, and told me they only had five cents to make it. Reading it, I thought it could lead one either to cynicism or adventurous-ness. When the old woman, the heroine of *Late Call*, goes to live in her son's new-town house, her sense of alienation, of something going on in her mind, makes her remember her childhood within a cottage in a village, a backwater, during the long drought of the first dozen years of this century.

The guillotine hanging over me about the cost of the sets actually helped me bring the past and the present together. The way you think you know about the past is like the way you remember a dream on waking; the bits of the room which you happen to have fallen asleep in can somehow obtrude into that dream when you wake. You're left with a lingering image of the dream, and yet you have your waking sense of the room – that's the window, that's the chair, that's where I am. So I set all the [1911] scenes among the modern furniture in the living room of this new-town house. It could be the solution, or it could be simply the acceptance of the fact that that's the way people think about the past. I don't know – nobody knows.

Not one critic, not one letter, not one telephone call to the BBC – nothing. Nobody noticed, either because that *is* the solution to the way people think about their past – in the context of where and who they are now – and they accepted it, or . . . well, if I dwell upon why there was no response it might make me cynical. But that was the pattern of the series. X number of cheapo, cheapo sets – five or six, no more. It was as basic as that. It was probably made for about £40,000, or less.

GF: *Did you feel you were able to invest it with some of your own themes?*
DP: I don't know. In a way that would be a betrayal. What is more interesting is if that other ground that someone has occupied happens here and there to nudge something in the top right-hand or left-hand corner of yourself. Then it's more likely a so-called adaptation will work.

GF: *Did you initiate* Casanova?
DP: Yes. Like most people I thought of the popular image of Casanova. I had a weekly slot as a book critic on *The Times*, briefly, and one thing that came in was a new translation of his memoirs. I thought, 'Oh, that's interesting. That's something one might write about.' But of course as soon as I said that I had to stop reading them, and I never reviewed them because, as a writer, I didn't want to know too much.

GF: *Did you abandon the memoirs as you got into writing the series?*
DP: Yes. The credits say it was 'based on' them but that's crap. I had a list of his dates, when he was in prison, when he escaped, how he ended, and the details of some of the women, but that was about it. Most

15  *Casanova*: Frank Finlay

memoirs are self-serving and adorned with lies and I thought his were probably the same.

GF: *Your Casanova is similar to the protagonists of some of your other plays in that he has a certain disgust for the way sexual desire asserts itself over spirituality.*

DP: I assumed Casanova must have had that thing they biologically refer to as '*tristitia post coitum*' – the sadness after fucking. And since he was also locked up, I drew together the moment of his death in a castle in Germany and, in his memory, the moment of his escape from the prison in Venice. I made them the same point because even if, like Georges Simenon, he had penetrated 10,000 women, or however many it was, that was a very obsessive and driven thing to have had to do – and there must, therefore, be some need for release and relief from the obsession. Those are my thoughts on it, coming from puritanism, I think, as a strand of thought. Puritans are fornicators too, but I think they could place obsessive sexual behaviour in the same context as eating and defecating, which like every bodily function is troubling to a genuine puritan.

GF: *You contributed an adaptation of Thomas Hardy's* A Tragedy of Two Ambitions *to the* Wessex Tales *series in 1973, and your seven-part* Mayor of Casterbridge *went out in 1978. What drew you to Hardy?*

DP: The wonderful descriptions of the West of England, the care for little scenes – people looking out of a window and seeing the fair, or somebody doing a job, which will then be described without any of that English condescension – and that way he has of constantly winding the wheel to make fate conspire against human emotions. You know Hardy's characters are in danger the moment they fall in love or struggle to express something really deep and moving; that something is going to happen to swat them down. As a prose writer, Hardy's world picture is not even remotely close to mine. He was an atheist and a pessimist who was driven by other beasts, if you want to call them that, than the beasts that drive me.

GF: The Mayor of Casterbridge *is driven by superstitions and local vil-lage tittle-tattle – that inward-lookingness that you'd explored in the* Forest of Dean *in your* A Beast with Two Backs.

DP: Yes, and which was the same in almost any rural area. Partly because he had such a bleak mind Hardy was able to describe what that really does mean. In a small community Voice A will say, 'Did you know . . .?' Voice B will say, 'You'll have to prove it,' and Voice C will pass it on as truth. A person can be *flayed* that way.

GF: *The Mayor of Casterbridge* is *about grave truths not being told, isn't it?*
DP: And the long, unravelled consequences of a drunken, shameful, one-act play set in the morning, as it were – the long, long reverberation which nothing one does can prevent. Sooner or later it's going to rise up and smack you down.

GF: *Do you feel when you adapt a book into drama that you have to stay true to its spirit? I once asked this question of Ruth Prawer Jhabvala and she gave me a resounding no.*
DP: I think you do have to stay true to the spirit – the spirit that you hear when you are reading a book, whatever it is that that triggers. Prose has a capacity to trigger a whole series of *under* images – that's what reading is, and it has enormous power. There is a description somewhere of the various ways in which various people read Arthur Ransome in their childhood. One reader said, 'I used to read all my books in a chair, or in a room with everyone around, but for *Swallows and Amazons* I had to get behind the settee or the sofa and read it like that.' Those things continue to resonate. Often you'll be reading a piece of fiction and it will spiral into some of your own memories and perceptions, because that's what it's like to read. The strong pictorial image of words on a page, if properly and powerfully enough composed, can push you into your own mind – even as you take in what you're reading.

I think the ideal adaptation is a relationship between a work of prose and a screenwriter made up partly of awe and partly of colonization. There is Keats's image of standing on a hill in a new world, which is the *book*; and there is also what you bring from the old world as a reader.

GF: *Reading a book is a unique experience for each reader because you supply your own images when you read. It's a simplistic notion, but it's exactly what separates that experience from seeing a film, where the images are prescribed.*
DP: That's why 'adaptation' is a dangerous word. Literal transliter-ations of books never work. *The Great Gatsby* [film: 1974] was literal, and as a result it failed to get in and among what it was like to read the book.

GF: *What is the difference between the way* Gatsby *was done and the way you adapted* Tender is the Night?

DP: I adapted the book in the same way that I would have read it – that is, I would say, 'Yes, I like this book, I am impressed by it, I feel this or that degree of pleasure and amazement, awe, whatever, about the prose describing these people at this time.' First I'm reading it; but also it is intruding, obtruding, nudging, pushing, whispering to me about things that I know about my own life, and that's what makes it work as a drama. That's what a novelist would wish of his or her own readers. I wanted to keep some of that going, some of my own feelings in there, without colonizing Fitzgerald's territory, which I wouldn't have the impertinence to do anyway. But it would have been far more of a dis-service simply to plunge into it, because those two media – the novel and drama – are so different.

GF: *Particularly as Fitzgerald's prose is so specific.*

DP: Yes. And that's the thing – you can only show it in another way. You're translating your responses, your feelings, but you're also, as a duty, trying to say, 'This is what the book was like to *me*.' When you translate Pushkin from Russian to English, that wonderful, simple Rus-sian is easily lost, unless you show something that is not just an invi-tation, but a *living in* the way Pushkin writes.

GF: *An adaptation is never going to be perfect for everyone, simply because no two readers interpret a book in exactly the same way. Every-one's going to have their mental image of Jay Gatsby and Dick Diver.*

DP: A few of them might have – but Fitzgerald, the poor sod, died almost forgotten in that sense, with a few thousand readers at most. With a television series you're talking about millions of viewers.

GF: *You followed the later version of* Tender is the Night.

DP: Yes. The reason Fitzgerald wrote it again was because he knew he hadn't got it right. He kept trying to change it, partly because anxieties about writing had already entered his soul. It's a bit like going into the cutting room when you think you've got something wrong and using the editing as a chance to change it. But if you change it, you might end up with something even more wrong. In a sense that's what Fitzgerald was doing. People say Hollywood destroyed him, but he'd been in film for years. I think it's too easy to say that films did this or that to him; almost precisely the opposite is true.

16  *Tender is the Night*: Peter Strauss as Dick Diver

GF:  Tender is the Night *was co-produced by the BBC and the American cable network Showtime, with Australia's Seven Network and 20th Century-Fox also involved. How did you negotiate your way through all that?*

DP:  The BBC said to me, 'We've got this deal with Showtime. Can you do it in five episodes?' I looked at it and said, 'No, I can't do it in five. I'll do it in six.' They said, 'Well, you talk to them.' And on one of my trips to America I talked to someone at Showtime and explained my reasons, and that was it – we did it in six. I'd thought, 'The BBC will sit in between me and them; I'm just going to relate to the BBC – never mind Showtime.' But of course Showtime did exert an influence and it wasn't what it should have been. I'll say no more.

GF:  *It was the first thing you'd done for television for five years. Did the time you'd spent in America influence your writing of it in any way?*

DP:  It's very difficult to work out what 'America' means. Nobody had ever tampered – as I would put it, with a very prejudiced point of view; creatively influenced would be another way of putting it – with my work in England. But in America the imperative of taking the audience with the narrative drive, taking the audience with you – what does the first act mean, the second act, the third act? – all that language is moot. Some of it must have rubbed off on me. I've got four scripts out there now, variously waiting for what may or may not be a green light – 'forever amber' is probably a more accurate description of where they'll stay.

All your experiences affect the way you write. Since my two experiences of directing I almost feel a hatred for the writer – i.e. myself. If you hang around long enough, and you do enough things and are friendly with enough people, you will undoubtedly be influenced by imperatives from outside your own culture, by commercial imperatives, and in my case particularly by the acknowledgement of the fading-away of a certain television culture. Good or bad, all those things have an effect on the way you address narrative. I have noticed that my scenes are getting shorter. When I am writing a script for America I get worried now if a scene goes over a page, because I know what they expect. So there must be some pressure in my mind to keep it short. That can be negative or positive; generally speaking it's a negative influence. But if you seek to live and work within a *variant* of popular culture it's something you need to know – something *I* needed to know.

GF:  *Was writing for the movies something you needed to do?*

DP: I don't know. I've always had an ambivalent relationship with popular culture, which is partly expressed in *Pennies* and a few other things. There is some sense in which I have been Arthur Parker myself, attempting to escape some of those rigidities of the English class system through demotic, popular drama. To achieve that within a film culture you need the direct injection of the truly crude, commercial, capitalist, money-orientated Hollywood culture, sometimes as a straight hit into the vein. That's what it *probably* did for me. I don't know. I don't actually want to assess it. But I know that everything you do leads somewhere.

GF: *When you read Christabel Bielenberg's* The Past is Myself *what did you see in it that would enable a new perspective on the war, apart from the obvious idea of an Englishwoman living in Nazi Germany?*
DP: I had read a review of the book in *The Economist* several years before and there was something about the review that made me want to get hold of the book. It was out of print, but I got a copy published in Ireland, and then I decided to try and get the rights, for a couple of reasons. It was a story about married love in a way that was unselfconscious. It was the kind of writing that people who haven't written write, an unadorned, straightforward narrative, with a simplicity that left a great deal unsaid. It also felt like the Second World War in a matchbox, in that the great events surged around and beyond the story, and the domestic and the personal became paramount.

I started with two strong prejudices – one against that class of English person, and one against the Germans – and both seemed to me to be well and truly countered by this particular account. But there was probably a deeper need for me – as an act of writerly hygiene, if I can put it that way – just to do a piece of naturalistic, straightforward, unadorned, chronological narrative. It was like washing my brain under the tap, a feeling that I needed to do that sort of thing now and again.

I found it very difficult to write, partly because there was a real person out there who could read and comment upon the script – she had that right. Also, I didn't want to intrude in any way. And although I had to invent things and had to tailor and chop, I took the opportunity to try and make each scene a bit like a soap, in a way, but full of reality and economy. Whether that came off or not I don't know, but it was out of that complex of reasons that I thought I wanted to do it.

GF: *Did Christabel Bielenberg have rights of consultation?*
DP: Yes. She had been approached by many people in the past, including

some American companies, to sell the book, and under her very precise questioning people had seemed to indicate to her the kinds of things they were going to do with it, which she didn't want; she didn't need the money. She met me in a hotel in London. I talked to her, and she cross-examined me and said at the end, 'Well, I've decided that I'm going to trust you.' So I took that trust on.

GF: *Did she know of your work?*
DP: Very little, because she and Peter, her husband, live in the part of Ireland beyond the reach of the BBC. I don't think they watch television too much. Being a typically thorough elderly lady, however, she'd made inquiries and was prepared. And when I sent her the script she obviously had things to say, some of which I had to resist, and explain why. She attended the first rehearsal and came down on location one day.

GF: *As you wrote it, were you attempting to filter Christabel's story through her naïvety?*
DP: Yes, in the sense of political naïvety and personal values, in that she says very early on, 'What have politics to do with people like us?' And also in the sense of her being wealthy and marrying a wealthy German and being apolitical – not, as it were, indifferent to the fate of people, but indifferent to their fate as expressed in political jargon, which is the way that many bourgeois and upward German people saw the whole phenomenon of Nazism. They saw something in the rise of the Nazi Party that was distastefully beyond them, almost as much for social as political reasons. And then of course came the gradual realization, which never comes all at once in any of our lives, that politics are important – the crisis for Christabel being the clash between two nationalities, which was very much stronger then than it is now. So I began with her wedding and her father really making a last-minute plea for her not to marry a German.

GF: *You chose not to engage with the Holocaust at all?*
DP: The only public event it engages with is the burning of a synagogue when Christabel and Peter are driving home from the dance. There is the bombing, of course, and Christabel takes in a Jewish couple, warned by her husband's colleagues that because he was engaged in the Resistance she was putting everything at risk by doing this. But when it came to the personal moment, the crisis, she simply had to do it.

GF: *You show Christabel's insulation from the war beginning to break down in small, quotidian events.*

DP: You see her gardener teaching her kids to 'Sieg Heil!' triumphantly in front of her, and changing into his brownshirt uniform in the garden shed. When her children run out of the kindergarten and the younger one shows her the postcard they've been given of Hitler and says, 'The teacher says he's the greatest man who ever lived,' she cannot, obviously, say, 'No, he isn't.' It's dangerous to assume anything, but I was assuming that people knew the main public events, so I ended episode one with the declaration of war, but then kept to Berlin and the Black Forest, showing the war through the changing life around them. That's why I say, without parody, 'Second World War in a matchbox'. I hate all those Second World War films and attempts to re-create the large-scale public events. When every perception is changed, what doesn't change is, 'How would *you* behave in this situation, even if you started in the most privileged position possible?'

When I did need to show a big event – such as the fall of Paris – I had Christabel and Peter at the cinema, watching it on a newsreel. There are brief shots of the German entry into Paris, with this triumphant voice-over, and then Hitler appears on the screen and the audience starts to cheer and clap. Then 'Deutschland über Alles' is played and everyone has to stand up, and Christabel is looking at Peter, and asking herself, 'Is he singing too proudly? Is he too German at this moment?' The public is, as it were, oblique. A similarly sidelong glance.

My question was: how would all this affect comfortably-off people, who are gradually stripped even of that, so that Peter ends up in a concentration camp and Christabel is lonely and scared in the Black Forest, volunteering to give an interview to the Gestapo? She does it, in fact, with tremendous upper-class English panache; when she comes into the room at the camp and the German turns those bright lights on her, she says, 'Switch those lights *off*!' – and lo and behold, he does.

GF: *The marriage survives through the war and is obviously a symbol of strength. Was it a departure for you to depict a much happier marriage than you usually do?*

DP: Have I shown unhappy marriages? Yes, I suppose I have, from time to time. Well, it was a departure, and I didn't want to get trapped in my own little box of tricks. As I say, it was sort of an act of hygiene. That was my personal motive – apart from the desire to look at the politics, that time, the way people felt, and the wish to balance the picture against

17  *Christabel*: newsreel of the Germans entering Paris
18  *Christabel*: Christabel (Elizabeth Hurley) and Peter (Stephen
Dillon) – the sidelong glance

all those big, quasi-documentary analyses of the would-be drama of the war. I tried to get that spirit of a slightly naive, open, transparent way of speaking about her life. That's why I called it *Christabel* and focused it entirely upon her.

GF: *Do you generally find it harder to write naturalistically?*

DP: I found it hard to write because there was somebody real out there. When she wrote to me a couple of times I had a very peculiar feeling, as though one of my own characters was writing to me. There is a short story by L. P. Hartley which has a character from one of his stories writing to him; the postcards start from way off and the postmarks get nearer and nearer – it's obviously very threatening. That image did bob into my mind. But it was a healthy thing for me to do – that's the only way I can put it. If you're training for football or something, the trainer might say, 'Don't sprint, don't go up on the bars, don't do gymnastics – why don't you dribble the ball a bit?' That was the feeling I had as a writer. I don't know what people thought of the end-product, but every now and again one wants to do something like that. I just wanted to have a change.

# CHAPTER 4

# Serials with Songs

*Pennies from Heaven, The Singing Detective,*
*Lipstick on your Collar*

MARLOW: You are the girl in all those songs . . .
NURSE MILLS: What songs?
MARLOW: The songs, the songs. The bloody, bloody songs.
*The Singing Detective*

Potter's occupation of the inside of the head found its most evocative (and celebrated) expression in his non-naturalistic device of using cheap songs as 'chariots of ideas', first in the *Pennies from Heaven* serial (1978) and subsequently in *The Singing Detective* (1986) and *Lipstick on your Collar* (1993), which together form a trilogy about the mediating effects of popular culture in, respectively, thirties, forties, and fifties England. In these serials, characters do not burst into song, as in the classic Hollywood musical, but into a lip-synched rendition of songs whose lyrics and melodies usher in or echo a character's emotions. It is a complex notion that defeated the makers of the *Pennies from Heaven* film (1981) and the imitative Steven Bochko CBS series *Cop Rock* (1990). Although its mood approximated that of the serial, the Hollywood *Pennies* was a formal failure because the elaborate costuming and ritzy sets required each number to begin and end on cuts, breaking the flow of consciousness.

Crucial to Potter's concept is the seamlessness of the transition from conscious thought to song back to conscious thought: think of the songs as brightly lit fuses in the electrical current of the mind and you go some way to understanding their synaptic power – not to underplay their function as sources of comedy, lyric intensity and pathos.

Potter uses the songs in different ways in each of the three serials. *Pennies from Heaven*, set in 1935, the year of Potter's birth, is the story of a lower-class travelling song-sheet salesman, Arthur Parker (Bob Hoskins), whose sexually repressed wife (Gemma Craven) cannot satisfy his carnal needs. Arthur has bought into the banality and 'silver-lining' optimism of the songs he peddles, such as 'The Clouds Will Soon Roll By' and 'Roll Along Prairie Moon', but he is doomed by his idealistic belief in their sentiments and by his duplicitousness; on a reverse trajectory, Eileen (Cheryl Campbell), the Forest of Dean infant-school teacher he seduces, is able to tell fact from fantasy. She does not believe in the songs or really seek to make the world other than it is. In the scene where Arthur and Eileen are smashing records, it is Arthur's inability to break 'Roll Along Prairie Moon' that indicates he is weaker than Eileen.

In *The Singing Detective*, as the acerbic, self-pitying P. E. Marlow (Michael Gambon), a sufferer of psoriatic arthropathy, lies boiling in a hospital bed, his mind as lesioned as his body, the viewer is borne along on his childhood reveries and his sadomasochistic reworking of his twisting, third-rate pulp thriller about a crooning, debonair gumshoe. The source of Marlow's psychosomatic sickness is (as often with Potter) the memory of a primal act – he observed his mother's adultery in the forest when he was nine and revenged himself on her lover's backward son – which shocked him into emotional withdrawal, sex-loathing and misogyny. The songs arrive in his mind not as wishful epiphanies, as they do in Arthur's, but as unbidden hallucinations, harbingers of poison or poignant musings or memories; just as Marlow's feverish imaginings and journeys back to the past are psychological detective clues in his attempt to reconstruct what Potter calls the 'sovereign self', so the songs are floating signifiers. Meanwhile, the structural mosaic of *The Singing Detective*, which anticipated the dense narrative layers of the *Blackeyes* series, was complemented by Potter's most ambitious stratification of filmic styles, ranging from the hallucinatory *film noir* of the Skinskapes sequence to the soap operatics of the hospital scenes.

Potter returned to a linear narrative for *Lipstick on your Collar*, his first serial for Channel 4. Unfolding at the time of the Suez Crisis in 1956, *Lipstick* depicts Britain at a watershed, regretfully discarding its imperial past and on the cusp of social upheaval, symbolized by rock and roll and the drive towards acquisitive, materialistic values. The conflicts in the drama are generational and class-driven. National Serviceman Private Francis Francis (Giles Thomas), a gauche, humble, but Oxford-bound Russian-language clerk posted to the War Office, is bewildered by the public-school-derived military-speak and supercilious manners of the Whitehall wallahs – Lt-Col. Bernwood, Majors Church, Hedges and Carter – and finds an enemy in the uncouth, spit-and-polish career soldier Corporal Berry and an ally in the shortly to be demobbed Private Hopper. He also develops an idealistic infatuation with Berry's wife Sylvia (Louise Germaine), a mercenary blonde cinema usherette – as does the seedy, once-famous cinema organist Atterbow (Roy Hudd). As

Francis clumsily negotiates the two worlds, Hopper (Ewan McGregor), an aspiring rock drummer bored with the futile bureaucracy of the War Office, projects his musical fantasies on to reality: thus the ticking-off Major Church gives Francis for spouting a romantic Pushkin line at him turns into a lip-synched rendition of Frankie Vaughan's 'The Garden of Eden', with Bernwood, Church, Hedges and Carter, and their American colleague Colonel Trekker cavorting lewdly in front of the hapless Francis as a pin-up Eve fondles a penis-headed serpent in the foreground.

Later, Bernwood's breakdown (his nostalgic yearning for the past is invoked by the insinuating strains of a cinema organ, linking him to the fallen Atterbow) suggests to Hopper the Stargazers' 'I See the Moon', accompanied by a frenzied Ali Baba fantasy replete with balloons, belly-dancers, Arabs, a leering camel, the ubiquitous Eve, and an opportunity for the three young soldiers to pelt the officers with ordure. When 'normality' is restored and Bernwood continues with his perorations, he kicks a balloon, left over on the War Office floor, out of his way. That detail may have been supplied by *Lipstick*'s director Renny Rye, but it reinforces the notion that in Potter's work, as in all our heads, reality and fantasy ultimately have no boundaries.

The songs in *Lipstick* play a similar role to the songs-as-psalms in *Pennies*, but they have a harder, more comedic, and more sexual resonance, befitting the brash fifties: when the lovelorn Francis turns Sylvia into a bucolic fantasy figure in his head, Hopper, hearing a Platters song, endows her with the trappings of luxury – champagne, suspendered thighs and so on. As Potter brings his song-cycle up to mid-century, the Depression idealism of *Pennies from Heaven* and the melancholy post-war yearning of *The Singing Detective* have given way to a craving for affluence – a time when every young squaddie and every peroxide blonde might dream of having it as good as, in time, Harold Macmillan would say they did.

GF: *In the first two series you wrote,* Casanova *and* Late Call, *you cut backwards and forwards in time, memory and imagination. You would do that again in* The Singing Detective. Pennies from Heaven, *however, is completely linear. Was that dictated by the fact that you were for the first time, over the course of a series, bringing in songs, and wanted to avoid adding other strata, for simplicity's sake?*

DP: It was dictated by the nature of Arthur, I think. He lived in the present tense. If he had any past he'd lie about it. But you didn't really want to know about his past. There he was, a song-sheet salesman,

19  *Lipstick on your Collar*: 'I See the Moon' (Douglas Henshall, Ewan McGregor and Giles Thomas)

believing in the songs, believing in his own fantasies, his gift of the gab, his own lies. He was a cork on the water. You didn't need to see what was below the cork because the cork was always floating on top of it.

With other, more complicated characters, who are searching for something else, you need to know *why* they are searching, *where* they come from, *what* they are, *what* they think, *what* they believe. Because their beliefs have moral authenticity, even when they lose them or are in despair, they have some idea of what it is really like to believe, trust or hope something, as opposed to Arthur, who could actually believe in something given by popular culture like 'Roll Along Prairie Moon'. He was simple, and they aren't.

GF: *There are flashes of memory in* Pennies from Heaven. *There's the episode in the café, when Arthur – who's extolling his belief in the songs to the other salesmen – remembers being hit by a shell in the trenches.*

DP: But we don't know if anything Arthur *says* is true or not. We only know it's true when we *see* it happening to him. Even when he was most moved by Eileen, and scribbled his address down for her, he scribbled the wrong address. You meet people sometimes who seem utterly authentic; their eyes will moisten, the structure of their speech implies they really believe something, and for those minutes or seconds they might. But you have no idea *what* they believe because you have nothing to go on. They leave you anchorless. They are very difficult people to work out. They may be self-deluding or extremely self-*knowing*, but they have a paintbrush in their hands and they paint the scenery in around them to fit whatever it is they momentarily feel. And it seems authentic until you look at it and you think, 'Oh God, that's hogwash!' That's Arthur.

GF: *In your 1969 play* Moonlight on the Highway *your use of the Al Bowlly songs seemed to presage the use of cheap songs in* Pennies from Heaven. *Were you already thinking of how you might use songs in this way?*

DP: I was probably half-thinking of it; I often used song titles as *my* titles, for example. Noël Coward has talked about the potency of cheap music – it was that kind of thing. I knew there was energy in that sort of music, and I knew there must be a way of being able to use it in the way that I perceived people used it themselves, for example the way that they would say, 'Oh, listen, they're playing our song.' I was interested in the feeling that people have sometimes when they listen to music of the past, the way songs wrap themselves around whatever emotion you happened to be carrying when you first heard them, the way a song can infiltrate the mood of a group of people. If somebody is playing accordion music in a Paris street you know it conveys with it the smell of garlic and Gauloises, a sort of bitter-sweet, part-nostalgia, part-genuine physical response to music itself.

I knew there was something awaiting me in terms of the use of music directly. If you play a song as background music, although you are conscious of it, the tune never comes into the forefront in the way that I know it does for some people in real life. The problem with the way I was orientating myself towards *Pennies* was, technically, how to bring this music right up front – not just played in the background, not score music, not used as an editorial comment: how do I get it central?

The way I used the adult body in *Stand Up, Nigel Barton*, way back in 1965, was a kind of clue. I decided to make believe that Arthur Parker, the song salesman, was actually singing, and that therefore the people around him were actually singing. It was then the adventure started for me. That was the sort of device I could use: it was both alienating and yet the closest I could get to putting the music right smack in the middle.

Once you've got the music in the middle, you've got to know what to do with it. The American television series *Cop Rock* was a long way from what I was trying to do, because first of all the music was new music, and secondly it seemed to be a comment upon the scenes. In *Pennies* the music didn't come out of a character situation as instinctively as a speech would have done, and it wasn't a comment upon the speech. It shifted the scene. It was in the head of the character, and although it might have been Al Bowlly's or Sam Browne's voice, it was actually that character's thoughts. And it wasn't an interlude, it wasn't added on, it was part of the drama. Even if the characters were singing in the scene and moving the scene, as though they were still in the story, it didn't allow the drama to stop.

GF: *It wouldn't have worked either, would it, if the characters had sung the songs themselves?*

DP: No, because these were genuine artefacts from the past that had been cannibalized and transformed into the workings of the head. If the characters had genuinely sung them it would have been a musical. The surrounding dialogue could have remained exactly the same, but the whole effect would have collapsed. This is the mystery. The thing that intrigues and puzzles and delights me is that the found object, the real thing, like a table and a chair, did the work for me, because I allowed it to.

GF: *So the songs, in effect, became part of Arthur's, or whoever's, stream of consciousness – or unconsciousness?*

DP: Yes, except I don't know what sort of label or description to give to it. It was a very difficult thing to do, trying to find the right songs from the hundreds I played. The inclusion of those songs had to be *written*. In one of his pieces Jorge Luis Borges has an imaginary author rewriting *Don Quixote* word for word, but it's still a different book. That's the way I felt.

GF: *You have described these cheap songs as like latter-day psalms.*

DP: I meant that partly ironically. They are our diminished *nod-back* to the psalms, but they are only *like* them in the sense that most popular tunes are saying the world is other than it is, or simpler than it is, or are bemoaning lost love. The Psalms of David can sound very paranoid even when they are aching with love for God. There's a huge gap, obviously, between the psalms and those songs, but their function is not dissimilar. It's the idea of the world shimmering with another reality, which is what 'Button up your Overcoat', or 'Love is Just around the Corner', or 'Down Sunnyside Lane' are saying with their cute, tink-tink-tink syncopations. They are both ludicrous and banal, reducing everything to the utmost simplification, but also, at the same time, saying, 'Yes, there is another order of seeing, there is another way, there is another reality.' It is this that makes karaoke, in an odd sense, popular too. It offers instant gratification, and instant stardom for those few minutes, but it's also about the world being other than it is. Singing is in a line of descent from the psalms, a way of puncturing reality, the ordered structure of things as they are. As soon as we start to sing, dance, remember, things are *not* as they are. We are no longer just gathering in the hay, as it were. It's a weird thing to do – a non-animal-like thing to do. The angel in us.

GF: *Was the Utopia yearned for in those songs of the thirties – which presumably were partly a response to the Depression and the slump between the wars – played out by the forties? Your use of songs in* The Singing Detective *was more knowing, the songs themselves less optimistic.*

DP: Well, it's grittier and harsher.

GF: *More melancholy, too, I think.*

DP: Yes, it's both. With something like 'It Might as Well be Spring' you have an old man singing a young man's love song, but it closed an awful lot of gaps between the old man and the young. You saw him as a young man, and you also saw, in a sense, how ludicrous the young man's falling in love was. All love has its own shape, and everyone ages and sickens and dies, and love, too, does the same, in that romantic sense. So a romantic song coming from a very old man's slack mouth tells you something about the old man, tells you something about romantic love. But it's also a good song, so you get a bonus!

GF: *Did the structure of* The Singing Detective *dictate that you had to use fewer songs?*

DP: No, I was using the songs differently. *The Singing Detective* is much more complicated than *Pennies from Heaven*. In *Pennies* Arthur Parker, believing in the songs in his simple-minded kind of way, had licence, as it were, to inject those songs everywhere and in any way, and make them seem real. In *The Singing Detective*, Marlow, sick, trying to reassemble himself, was resisting them, didn't believe in them, or only believed in them in the way he believed in his cheap thrillers. The songs played the same kind of function as his story, his cheap detective novel, which sneaked up on him and revealed to him how much of his own life was in them; how much of his own misogyny and self-pity and his own inner myth was bound up with this cheap writing. In *Pennies* the songs were believed in by the character. In *The Singing Detective* they were hard little stones being thrown at Marlow. Arthur's tragedy was that he was throwing them out *to* the world. He could never assemble himself, he wasn't capable of that, and although there was a certain shape to his life it was one that he could never get hold of; the songs prevented him getting a hold of it. In *The Singing Detective*, the cheap fiction, the illness and the cheap songs – well, not so cheap – were together conspiring to force him to recognize what he was: stark, stripped down, with nothing but a ferocious rhetoric, plus self-pity. Because the pain was so great he was trying to think of 'The Singing Detective' novelette that he had written, and trying to rewrite it simply as an exercise in not going mad. That in turn led him to start assembling his life, and the songs were part of that assemblage. Bu they were being resisted. They were not in any shape or form the way that Arthur saw the songs.

GF: *To be very literal about* Pennies from Heaven, *there seems to be no*

*kind of moral order, inasmuch as Arthur is hanged for a crime he didn't
commit.*

DP: No, but he had committed various crimes, and it was like a lurid
melodrama in that sense. But also, he comes back at the end. It was a
cheap form of a Christian structure. And it was showing how a simple
and weak man nevertheless still drew strength from what were simple
and weak myths. It was the power of the mythologies, really, that I was
dealing with. The morality is very clear, but it's not for me to explicate it
in any way. I would start being didactic if I did that.

There was a feeling, at the end, that *Pennies* was a parable, a kind of
morality tale in which the music and Arthur's weakness were the engines.
The only good thing about Arthur, even though he was an adulterer and
a liar and was weak and cowardly and dishonest, was that he really
wanted the world to be like the songs, as he explained them, or tried to
explain them in his less than articulate way. There was something that he
was responding to, and although it was cheap and banal and all those
things, he nevertheless had that part of himself which was responding to
a myth of a kind, which was wanting the world to be other than or better
than it was, and therefore wanting himself to be better than he was. He
couldn't quite manage it, but it was at those moments when he came
alive. Those were the moments that were a kind of epiphany for him, a
kind of blessing, even though he was made to suffer for it. When you
have an inadequate system of beliefs, or if it's too flimsy to bear the
weight, it will collapse, and it collapsed upon him. But the yearning for it
was important.

GF: *He's a very ambiguous character anyway. The most frightening
scene in the whole series is when he's standing in the cornfield and the
blind girl has gone on her way, and he says he would do anything if he
could make her see again, and then he makes a crude sexual remark
about her.*

DP: That's right. His instant emotion was there, and then that sexuality
was there. He couldn't deal with his emotions at all. There are lots of
people like that.

GF: *Eileen's trajectory is very discomfiting. She starts out as a virginal,
sweet-natured Forest of Dean schoolteacher and ends up as an opportun-
istic tart and a murderess.*

DP: And yet, through that, she remains the stronger one, the one who,
oddly, is more in touch with her feelings. Even though she has her outs,

20  *Pennies from Heaven*: Bob Hoskins as the song salesman
Arthur Parker

21 *Pennies from Heaven*: Cheryl Campbell as the Forest of Dean schoolteacher Eileen

she does things that Arthur couldn't even contemplate doing; Arthur will moralize about them, because that's part of the humbug he is, whereas she accepts the necessity of doing them.

GF: *Do you consider* Pennies from Heaven *a hopeful work? In naturalistic terms it's quite bleak – Arthur goes to the gallows – but then you resurrect him in a kind of coda.*

DP: But the coda, as you call it, is an intrinsic part of the whole thing. You can say lots of things are pessimistic, but are they? *The Singing Detective* was not bleak, in my opinion, in that it attempted to show accurately what it is like to be stripped of everything and then to attempt, via cheap fiction and a mix of memory – distorted memory, invented memory and real memory – to reassemble oneself. It was, in itself, a pilgrimage, an act of optimism that began with total nihilistic despair and ended with someone walking out into the world.

GF: *You talked earlier about the specificity of good art and you noted the banality of the lyrics and tunes of the cheap songs you use. There are clearly instances, however, where the lyrics of those songs are used in a specific way by you. For example, the psoriatic Philip Marlow muttering 'I've Got You under my Skin' in* The Singing Detective, *or the dreadful pertinency of 'I'd Be Lost Without You' from the title-song of* Cream in my Coffee, *as it applies to the elderly couple in that play.*

DP: It's never accidental. I choose the lyrics. I chose the tunes all through *Pennies from Heaven* and *The Singing Detective*, and have often used song titles, for example, for the titles of my plays, like *Moonlight on the Highway*, *Double Dare* and the 'angel plays' (*Angels Are So Few* and *Only Make Believe*). It's like an artist with 'objets trouvés'; they are genuine artefacts that you're picking up. But it's not serendipity. You're picking them up in order to use them. So, yes, it's part of the drama. It's as though you've written the tune yourself. That's what it feels like.

GF: *So you reclaim if for yourself?*

DP: You reclaim it in order to remake it. So it takes on the reverberations of all that is around it, and then those little lyrics start having added ironies.

GF: *In* Blade on the Feather *you pick up on the homosexual implication in 'The Eton Boating Song' in the scene where Cavendish and his butler sing it together with fond recall.*

DP: Maybe, but that was just a glance. It was also about English upper-classness. It was used with irony and comedy, and the scene built around it is supposed to be funny in a creepy kind of way. There were other things going on, too. It's the kind of humour which also shows the seeds of that very complicated notion of betrayal I was playing with in *Traitor*.

GF: *Did you think you'd exhausted the device of characters lip-synching songs after* The Singing Detective?
DP: I thought I had after *Pennies*, nearly ten years earlier! There's something about using songs as chariots for ideas. I have to be very careful not to turn it into an automatic response. That's one of the reasons I did *Christabel* and two novels after *The Singing Detective*. Until it seemed inevitable that I should use music in that sort of way again, I certainly had no plans to do so. As long as it's not done by rote, and as long as it's not done because people expect it, then that will be all right. Maybe.

GF: *You rewrote quite a lot of* The Singing Detective?
DP: Yes. I had lots and lots of chats with the director, Jon Amiel, and obviously he was responding in his way to the material. In between all that, or because of all that, I became aware that I was holding back on something, some sharpness – it needed to be more honest – and Jon's very good at pushing stuff at you or pulling stuff from you, perhaps a bit of both. But I knew if I started changing Scene A and Scene G, say, then it wouldn't be A and G that would change, it would be A to Z, so I decided I would redo them all.

GF: *What did you change?*
DP: I made Marlow suffer more. I made him more bitter at the beginning, and I made his relationship with his wife stronger, but I also allowed her to attack his evasion in using his illness both as a defence and as a form of attack rather than addressing what was really going on. Small changes in scenes here, there and everywhere would gradually become more dominant, so I would have to rewrite what was around them as well and rethink the emotional trajectory of it. That's what happens in genuinely creative discussion, where you know it's not going to be taken out of your hands – i.e. it's not going to be done by a studio that's going to buckle and twist it out of your concept of its shape. So you have the self-confidence of knowing that you can sit down and re-do things – not in the sense of patching-and-mending, according to a corporate philosophy, but in order to get out of it what you half buried in it,

and maybe pull out even more in some way. Jon said he nearly wet himself when he read the rewrite, because there we were in pre-production and suddenly everything seemed different. But of course it wasn't all different. It just had much more punch and power, and he had to roll with it then.

GF: *Did you enhance the* film noir *quality of the singing detective sequences, especially at the beginning of episode one?*
DP: That probably got enhanced slightly, simply because it's an attractive style. It's darkness, if you like. The narrative drive element of the detective part, as well as its tone, was an emotional cousin to the other bits. It could sweep them up and allow access to the childhood and to the real emotions, because they had to be encased by this pained, bitter, sardonic, side-of-the-mouth, quipping delivery of the detective of pulp fiction. So the two elements started becoming gloves – you put your hands in either. The serial form allows the freedom to discover such a space. You have the time and you have the rhythm of many different narratives, which you couldn't have in single pieces. That's probably where I made the mistake in some of my single plays – in *Secret Friends*, say, where the complications became evident complications, whereas they needed to be teased out. They probably needed another form in order to be best expressed.

GF: *In a multi-tiered or stratified work like* The Singing Detective *there are a number of different routes that allow the viewer to get into it.*
DP: They are not 'provided', in that sense, but if you go down one you will meet the other. They're not alternative routes; they're more like a maze, except that each step you take inevitably bumps you against the step you would have taken had you gone somewhere else.

GF: *I believe you had wanted to shoot the hospital scenes on video in the electronic studio?*
DP: I originally had a couple of meetings with Jonathan Powell and set it up myself by talking to him. The cost of doing a serial was then – as it still is, but then even more so – a big issue. I knew that the bulk of the scenes in the 'present tense' was going to take place in the hospital ward – that is, I didn't know it for sure, but my instinct was that that was where the real struggle was going on. Technically there was no reason, since it was all on one set, why it couldn't be shot on video. That would have had a big effect on the cost, because you were talking about at least

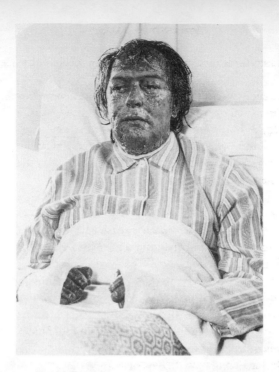

22–24    *The Singing Detective*: Michael Gambon as Philip Marlow
(hospital patient, gumshoe and crooner)

four hours' worth of drama, which structurally was like the drama of my early plays.

But the match between video and 16-mm. film never works. It might have been interesting, because the mismatch could have also been an emotional one, but in the end everybody wants to use film. Jon obviously did, and that decision was made very early on, and without any struggle from me. It was made by the process, by the fact that the money was there if we agreed to do it all on 16-mm, which we did.

GF: *On a more general level, have you been able to relinquish the idea of writing for the electronic studio and the sense of interiority it affords?*

DP: That's something I accepted long ago. You fight a battle until you lose it, and then you step sideways. What you do is retain the virtues, or as many as you can, of what used to be. Some of the scenes of *The Singing Detective* were thirty or forty pages long. Normally in a movie a scene is two pages to two-and-a-half pages, or at the most three or four. But you can get three or four scenes on a page. Sometimes that's necessary; it happens in *The Singing Detective*, for example, and it certainly happens in the screenplays that I've done. But what I want to attend to is the natural shape and rhythm of a particular scene. If it takes twenty pages, it takes twenty pages, and that's something I will not compromise on. Read my lips.

GF: *You denied in interviews at the time of* The Singing Detective *that Marlow was in any sense autobiographical, but subsequently you've said you were less certain about that.*

DP: There's overt autobiography, which is first-person narrative. That says, 'In 1959 I did this, in 1962 I did that, and this is what I felt, these are the facts.' There is also another kind of autobiography, which is fictive and uses the experiences and the geography and the memories of how one felt about certain kinds of things, like illness and geographic dislocations in childhood – in my case, moving from the Forest of Dean to London, briefly, and then back. There are *real* memories that are invoked millions of times even if you are writing about Julius Caesar.

The *form* of autobiography is very powerful because it appears to be authentic. As I've said before, autobiography is one of the most venal and lying of all the sub-art forms in prose. You could say that using real feelings was autobiographical, but in my opinion it isn't, because the narrative is driven by invention. None of the story and none of the relationships in *The Singing Detective* are mine, not the mother, the wife, not the kind of head that could have written a pulp detective story. Even those songs – half of which I hate –

GF: *Do you really hate them?*
DP: Yes, a lot of them I do, but it's sometimes the ones that I hate most that can give me the most traffic, simply because I become aware of saying to myself, 'Why the hell is it in my head then?' or, 'How can I bear to listen to it again?' But when you've got to find a lot of numbers you're going to have to hear a lot of drivel. The purpose is not to *illustrate* with a song, but to use the song as though it had just been written for that occasion – in other words, to turn the song into quasi-autobiography, as though I *had* written the song, which is to re-see, re-hear what may be an extraordinarily banal tune and nonsensical lyric. In other words, to give the song the meaning of the emotional and physical surround out of which you are made to re-hear it.

GF: *You were offended initially when people concluded, because of Marlow's illness, that he was some kind of spokesman for yourself.*
DP: No, I don't think that 'fictions' should ever have spokesmen for the writer. But just as nostalgia is a means to turn it inside out, so the conventions of apparent autobiography are very strong as a form, as a genre, so if people think, 'Oh, that's about him,' then in using it as a mode of story-telling you're already a long way along a certain road. What happened in *The Singing Detective* was that, rather than use an illness I knew nothing about, I used that particular one, and places I knew. But the details within that are a million miles away from me.

GF: *Given all the references to British culture in* The Singing Detective, *were you surprised that it was so well received in America?*
DP: I am amazed that anybody in America should even have begun to watch or even approve of *The Singing Detective*. I would have thought so many of the lines and jokes just could not travel, and they probably didn't. One of the troubles with the British film and television industry, as it attempts to internationalize itself, is that it assumes that it's got to genuflect towards other cultures. I don't believe that's true for one moment. I think that what travels is what is felt and observed to be true in itself. So I am going to make not the smallest concession to American taste, acting, personnel, images or language, because I think that's the wrong way to do it.

GF: *You are a writer/producer on* Lipstick on your Collar. *Have you been able to reconcile yourself to standing down as director?*
DP: Yes, reluctantly. But the pain of that has been considerably reduced by my finding a somewhat kindred spirit in Renny Rye, the director, who has done it brilliantly. I am delighted with him.

GF: *Once again you've gone back to a series of themes that you've looked at before, in this case with* Lay Down Your Arms, *a single play from 1970 which also showed a naïve young Russian-language clerk turning up at the War Office at the time of Suez. When you revisit old ground, is it to refine those ideas you were interested in before or is it using it as a new leaping-off point?*
DP: It's a new way. It just happened to be a coincidence of the place and the time. I think the entry of this young soldier is about the same in the two pieces, in my memory. But they are about utterly different things. They are not remotely the same piece of work.

GF: *Several of the characters in* Lipstick *bear similarities to those in* Lay Down Your Arms. *Francis, Hopper, Hedges with his braces and smirk, Bernwood with his melancholia – they each have their antecedents.*
DP: Do they? I wouldn't be surprised, because I have a memory of certain people in the War Office, and they probably occurred to me again, but I didn't look at *Lay Down Your Arms* again.

GF: *The fantasy elements within the numbers tend to be more extreme than in* The Singing Detective.
DP: There was more licence to do so within this structure and within this musical, so the numbers are more inventive.

GF: *What was the budget of* Lipstick?
DP: It was just under £1 million an episode.

GF: *Is that par for the course for an hour of British television drama now?*
DP: I think it was a bit more than usual because of the music numbers and because of the period setting. It was more expensive than, say, GBH, but then there's a lot more going on in it. There was a huge cast, lots and lots of dancers and bigger design costs as a consequence of production numbers. It was like making a musical, actually.

GF: *Your characters in* Lipstick *lip-synch to a mixture of fifties stan-dards and early rock 'n' roll songs – Jerry Lee Lewis, Elvis Presley, the Platters etc. – some of which continue to be played on the radio. Because they haven't receded quite so far into the past, does that mean they play a different role than the thirties songs in* Pennies *and the forties songs in* The Singing Detective?

DP: They do play a different role, but there is a kind of hidden agenda. Because the songs are abutting on to the recent past, because they have a more contemporary feel, they are more dangerous. There are two tech-nically interesting things for me about *Lipstick*. You think the hero is Private Hopper, but it isn't; it's Private Francis, the new National Serviceman in the War Office, but all the songs come from Hopper, every single one of them. Using two main characters enabled me to keep the narrative simple. I think, in some ways, *Lipstick* outdoes *Pennies* and *The Singing Detective*, because there's a lot let loose in it, but it's an absolutely linear structure, absolutely straightforward – there are no narrative complications, apparently. It doesn't make *those* sort of demands on you. It's all present tense.

GF: *There are momentary flashbacks in it.*

DP: But only to the day before, dabs of thought, as it were, within the same time-frame. I once said you should always look back on your past with tender contempt. Tender is important. The contempt is also important, but I don't mean hatred, I mean amusement, indulgence. A certain wincing ruefulness as well about just how wonderfully silly a very young man can be. Really, it's as simple as that.

GF: *Private Francis has an idealistic desire for the 'common' girl, Sylvia, who lodges upstairs in his aunt's house. His longing for her is not only idealistic, it's misplaced, because they're living on different planets.*

DP: It's a comic desire. He's comically idealistic, and yet carnal at the same time.

GF: *With Sylvia, did you want to get across that kind of bolshy, hard-edged female glamour of the fifties, the Ruth Ellis, Diana Dors-type peroxide blonde?*

DP: It's more like Diana Dors. She's quite an interesting character. She's trapped with a violent husband in a shitty little flatlet. She has the know-ledge that she's pretty, a certain ruthlessness that goes with it, but also an incapacity to get out of that situation. And she feels fugitive tendernesses

25   *Lipstick on your Collar*: Giles Thomas as Private Francis, the new boy in the War Office

26　*Lipstick on your Collar*: fantasist Private Hopper (Ewan
McGregor) and the 'common' Sylvia (Louise Germaine)
27　*Lipstick on your Collar*: director Renny Rye with Dennis Potter

and the self-knowledge that makes her tell Francis she won't have any-thing to do with him. She has tremendous resilience, all of which is caught and held in a quite marvellous way by Louise Germaine, who plays her.

GF: *The resentment between her and her landlady, Private Francis's Aunt Vickie, turns into a kindred feeling.*

DP: There's abuse going on between Sylvia and Aunt Vickie and Uncle Fred, the mad evangelist, and they are all exchanging insults all the time because they're living on top of each other. But Aunt Vickie does reach out in a female way to Sylvia, briefly. She is very soon rebuffed, mind you. But as Aunt Vickie says, 'It all comes down to the woman in the end.'

GF: *What's the significance of the Suez Crisis in all their lives?*

DP: Suez was Britain's last imperial gesture, and it failed because Big Daddy across the Atlantic said, 'No.' But at the same time the culture was changing, the music was changing. There was proto-rock coming in, a sense that the stuffy, regimented, bowler-hatted, brolly-toting, hier-archical, still stupidly half-imperialistic, greatly self-inflated England at the time was being broken up by plastics, colours, music. The consumer revolution was happening. The word 'teenager' was being used for the first time. Setting it during Suez made all that more explicit.

The songs in *Lipstick* are used to show that all those things were happening. You'll be in a big room in the War Office with these officers, and they're talking in that imperialistic way and have all these delusions and illusions. And yet they are also interesting people in their own right. The commanding officer, Bernwood, who goes round the twist, is a person who nevertheless moves you. So you see the Old England suffer-ing while these young privates claim their own place. Even though they've not got 'permission' to speak, as it were, they do manage to speak, in Hopper's case through the songs.

GF: *Bernwood has a nostalgia for those old cinema Wurlitzer organs that you talked about earlier as a memory from your childhood. He longs for the past, like so many of your other characters.*

DP: But he also has a worried feeling that, as he says, they've reached a time where every little black man and every little brown man opens his mouth and 'we' can't stand up to them any more. He has an utterly antediluvian attitude to Britain. Yes, he's got this other side to him, absent-minded, increasingly melancholy, increasingly feeling a sense of loss, his grip slackening on reality all the time. So it's just funny that in the same story there happens to be the last of the cinema organists still around – although it's a bit late, actually, for that. I thought it would be nice to let him enjoy the Wurlitzer or the Hammond or the Compton. People have all sorts of funny things in their heads.

GF: *Again, you're showing that kind of sweet pain for that which can't be recaptured.*
DP: And that includes the whole of the British imperial past, which is why Suez becomes such a big issue for these men.

GF: *Did you rewrite parts of* Lipstick *as it was being filmed?*
DP: Occasionally you have to. For instance, you might have to change the details around a production number, to get what the song is for. I had to do that with Bernwood's breakdown and the mad song that accompanies it, 'I See the Moon' by the Stargazers. I just made it clearer. Like adding a camel that shits.

GF: *Like Francis you served as a Russian-language clerk in the War Office. Does that period and the Suez Crisis resonate to you as a kind of coming of age for both yourself and post-war England?*
DP: I don't know. I was in my first term at Oxford at the time of Suez, so I was gone from there. The nine months I'd spent in the War Office was the last period of my National Service. Also, at age twenty you're growing, and obviously you hate the army. I was conscious that things were cracking in the social order – the very fact that I was going to Oxford was proof of that. I think it really is as simple as that. *Lipstick* is the story of two young men. It is the story of a nation at a moment of crisis. It is a story of change, and the music is illustrating living in the change. And there's a very strong narrative going on.

GF: *How did you draw the narrative strands together?*
DP: I just kept going with it. The two young men, Francis and Hopper, cross over their desires between the girl upstairs in the Fulham house and the niece of the American in the War Office. It's a comedy, really.

GF: *Although Suez – the threat of war – injects some seriousness into it.*
DP: Well, that gradually puts the boot down. Right from the beginning

you start thinking, 'Oh God, what's that feeling? It's on its way,' and
then that sense of utter delusion is sitting there.

GF: *But as Suez is resolved, and as Francis's relationship with Sylvia is
resolved, both anti-climactically, does a common thread emerge?*
DP: Only in what I've said before about change, and also what it's like
to be a young man. And those two young actors – Ewan McGregor
as Hopper, Giles Thomas as Francis – are played so very well that I
'remembered' more and more as the production went on.

GF: *How do the songs fit into the narrative structure?*
DP: They live within the change. You have the Prime Minister singing,
'You can do anything but don't step on my blue suede shoes,' which in
effect was what Eden was saying to Nasser! To show that music and to
be *in* that music while Suez is going on is a good example of how,
dramatically, the music can show what is happening in terms of the
breaking of the shell, or the fracturing of the egg, and some new, ugly
little chick coming out. What it is we don't know, but it isn't the old
England. It's a chick with blue suede shoes.

GF: *Was it harder to find the right songs than with* Pennies *and* The
Singing Detective?
DP: Harder only in the sense that I don't like fifties music very much, but
not really. Once you know where you're going, it narrows down the
options in terms of what the music could or couldn't be doing. And the
songs almost pop up in front of you. For example, Eden, the headlines in
the music papers and a young soldier, Hopper, thinking, 'Christ, they're
not going to let me be demobbed – they're going to keep me here,' all
suggested 'Blue Suede Shoes'. Because Hopper wants to be a drummer,
he's thinking about music all the time anyway. That's what it's like. So all
these things lead you to a certain choice and the number of songs available starts narrowing down.

GF: *Your use of the theme of* The Adventures of Robin Hood – *the
Richard Greene series – ushers in a nostalgia for the television of the
fifties.*
DP: It's a song I detest – there are so many of them! But it has a comic
value with those American voices, that rubbishy music, this silly image of
the past, and the fact that it was being played on what even then I was
still calling the wireless. It's a genuine artefact from the past, like a piece

of furniture. That was the sound that was in some people's heads some of the time – God help them.

GF: *What did you intend with the shepherd's homecoming fantasy? It's like a little fairy-tale.*
DP: It relates to Sylvia working as an usherette in the cinema and looking at the screen. It's a vulgar little fantasy out of her head – 'Oh, wouldn't it be nice . . .?' – the funny little gingerbread cottage, the sheep, the well, which has got a champagne glass on it. She's wearing what she thinks of as a peasant dress, and yet it's hitched up to make sure there's a stocking showing. And it's her dream of the movie kiss, and then of money. 'I sold the sheep,' he says. 'How much?' '£990,000.' She says, 'Oh, what a pity it wasn't a million,' which is exactly what Sylvia would have thought.

GF: *It punctures the idyll.*
DP: Yes, and yet it also retains it to a degree. She's living upstairs in this horrible little terraced house and yet can see these big, coloured birds, and the lovely little sheep, and the stork on the thatched roof and so on. It's funny in one way, but it's touching in another. The feeling of 'I want to get out of this grubby little place' is very much part of her mind.

GF: Lipstick *contains very little of that disgust or bile that you've sometimes poured out in your writing.*
DP: It's a very happy piece in many ways. It's a deceptive piece. There was more in the script than seems to be the case. I think what people will see in *Lipstick* is that outer carapace of authoritarianism and structured discipline that gradually gets punctured both by what is happening outside, and by the fact that you get into their heads. You start seeing that neither the officers nor the young men are ciphers. I could do this, I originally thought as I was writing it, with a live audience. It could almost be like one of those up-market chat-show things where you have a ring of people around. The genre that it is occupying for part of the time is that of the situation comedy. I just hope it's funny. I *think* it's funny. Even on the third take people were still laughing – at least, they seemed to be, inwardly. There has been a great deal of pleasure in the making of it. I think that was evident on the set. I am very pleased with it.

# CHAPTER 5

# Films and Stage Plays

*Pennies from Heaven, Brimstone and Treacle,*
*Gorky Park, Dreamchild, Track 29,*
*Sufficient Carbohydrate*

'It wasn't as bad as I thought it was going to be.'
Eileen in *Pennies from Heaven* (MGM)

Cinema is a director's medium which requires industrial compromise and specializes in the subordination of the writer. As a result, Dennis Potter's films have not so far yielded the fruits of his television drama. His move towards screenwriting was prompted, in any case, by British television's move away from videotaping plays in the electronic studio towards all-film drama in the late seventies. Potter's early television 'films' – including *Double Dare, Blue Remembered Hills, Blade on the Feather, Cream in my Coffee* – are not noticeable for their use of filmic technique, nor do they suffer from the homogenizing effects of movie production; but then in each of them Potter was well served in his directors, respectively John Mackenzie, Brian Gibson, Richard Loncraine and Gavin Millar. Loncraine was unable to repeat the trick with the Potter–Kenith Trodd film of *Brimstone and Treacle*: the references to the National Front in the play were omitted from the film because they wouldn't 'travel'; the studio-conscious and extremely funny effects whipped up by 'the devil' in the BBC production were replaced by bland fantasy sequences in the film.

In 1981, unable to raise British finance for his *Pennies from Heaven* screenplay, Potter launched the project at MGM with Herbert Ross as director and Steve Martin and Bernadette Peters replacing Bob Hoskins and Cheryl Campbell as the leads. Wishing to protect their property, MGM insisted that the *Pennies* serial should not be repeated on American television or sold to any other foreign territories. Potter and Trodd were obliged to buy back the BBC's copyright for $100,000, which exacerbated their already fraught relationship with the Corporation. In 1989 Trodd reacquired the serial rights from MGM for Alan Yentob at BBC 2, the actors' 'out-of-time' fees were settled, and the six-parter was shown in Britain for the first time since 1978.

Labouring under the illusion that *Pennies* was a musical, MGM borrowed $26 million to make their film version, expending it on elaborate sets and production numbers that wilfully diluted the purpose and the potency of Potter's cheap music, although he has contended that 'the religious element in the Hollywood *Pennies* is more accomplished'. For his efforts, Potter was rewarded with a then substantial £125,000 writer's fee, critical incomprehension (although Pauline Kael was a supporter), disastrous box-office, and an Academy Award nomination for Best Screenplay (based on material from another medium). Harold Pinter was nominated (for *The French Lieutenant's Woman*) in the same category that year.

Potter's *Unexpected Valleys* screenplay (about a ballet dancer torn between her career and motherhood) for Ross and two others for 20th Century-Fox were aborted before they reached production. Very little Potter can be detected in his adaptation of Martin Cruz Smith's Moscow thriller *Gorky Park* (1983). Directed by Michael Apted for Orion and starring William Hurt and Lee Marvin, the film became bogged down in production difficulties and emerged leaden and impenetrable. Much better were *Dreamchild* (1985) and *Track 29* (1987), which had their antecedents in, respectively, *Alice* and *Schmoedipus*. In Nicolas Roeg, director of *Track 29*, Potter found a kindred spirit: a filmmaker also interested in the way memory intermingles with the present. *Secret Friends* (1992), Potter's début as a feature director, is considered in the next chapter because of its thematic links to *Blackeyes*.

Potter's themes, motifs, use of old songs, and even his narrative structures have palpably influenced the Belgian filmmaker Jaco van Dormael, whose *Toto le héros* (1991) liberally borrows from *The Singing Detective*. Van Dormael shows an institutionalized curmudgeon borne back into the past as he seeks both to revenge himself on the neighbour who stole the girl he loves, Mark Binney-style, and to reclaim himself. Like the young Philip Marlow, the young Toto hankers to be a detective when he grows up; like *Pennies from Heaven*'s Arthur Parker, the grown-up Toto follows the woman of his dreams into a music shop. *Toto le héros* resembles over-exuberant *hommage* rather than grand larceny.

At the time of writing, Potter has two long-gestating films in pre-production. The first, under the auspices of Australian producer Lance Reynolds (David Bowie is attached as executive producer) is *Mesmer* with Roger Spottiswoode slated to direct Alan Rickman as the Austrian physician Franz Anton Mesmer. Renny Rye (*Lipstick on your Collar*) will direct Polly Walker in *Midnight Movie*, a Whistling Gypsy/BBC feature. Potter's highly original adaptation of D. M. Thomas's *The White*

*Hotel*, an American feature version of *The Singing Detective* (which at one time had Dustin Hoffman attached as star), and *The Mystery of Edwin Drood* (Dickens's unfinished novel completed by Potter in screen-play form) are not, as yet, 'go' projects.

Potter eschewed live theatre as a form early on in his career because of his belief in reaching the 'common culture' of television. He has written one play for the stage: *Sufficient Carbohydrate*, an adultery drama set on a Greek island and embodying a clash between British and American cultural values, which opened in Hampstead in 1984 before becoming a West End hit at the Albery Theatre after Potter, deeming it too preachy, had revised it. A revised version of *Vote, Vote, Vote for Nigel Barton* incorporating material from *Stand Up, Nigel Barton* was produced at the Theatre Royal in Bristol in November 1968; *Son of Man* was staged in Leicester in 1969 before transferring to the London Round House Thea-tre; *Only Make Believe* was staged in Harlow in 1974; *Brimstone and Treacle*, banned by the BBC in 1976, was first produced at the Crucible Theatre, Sheffield, in October 1977, and made its off-off-Broadway début at the Interart Theater in 1989.

GF: *You wrote* Sufficient Carbohydrate *for the stage and then adapted* Brimstone and Treacle *for theatre when the BBC banned it.*
DP: These were like holidays, or experiments, or fun, or the result of boredom. A writer should write, he should try these things. I could certainly write poetry, but no one will ever see that – or not while I'm alive, put it that way. Writing is writing, yes. Some forms are easier. I don't mean easier to do – but their grammar, their confidence, the place they occupy, is strong enough to allow you to do it. Some of them are in trouble, like the novel, but the theatre or drama can stay the course. But writing in these different modes is like jogging in the park – not that I would ever do such a disgusting thing – in that it limbers you up for what writing *is*.

GF: *You haven't written for theatre consistently – is that because part of you still wants to stay true to the idea of reaching a democratic audience?*
DP: I don't want to stay true to any ideas. I just want to write. But the form – whether it's theatre, film, television, an occasional novel, an occasional poem, whatever – they're all, when I do them, what I want to do. Otherwise I'm not staying true to anything. It's difficult enough to stay true to your personal relationships, let alone to your pen.

GF: *In* Sufficient Carbohydrate, *which was filmed as* Visitors *in 1987, you pit American brashness and vulgarity against British repression and aloofness, as you had done in* The Bonegrinder. *In* Track 29 *you deride American values, but at the same time there is this constant mining of American culture in your work. Your stance on America is double-edged.*

DP: Yes, it is ambivalent. I am aware, as Europe in particular and the world in general is compelled to acknowledge, that America was a rewriting of the book, if you like. It was the New World and all that that means. It has a genuinely populist culture, even though, as the other salesmen – expressing their English prejudice, which is both anti-Semitic and hierarchical – say to Arthur Parker in *Pennies*, 'Those songs? Come on Arthur. They're just written by Jew boys in green eyeshades.' But strip away that offensive way of putting it and, literally, that populist culture can be the result of someone sitting in an office, thinking, 'Does this work? Does that work? Will they like that in Peoria?' But it wasn't saying, 'Is this culture? Am I right?' It's a case, of 'There's the goods, do you want to buy them?' which few Europeans could say about their culture. I don't want to see European culture reduced to that, but neither do I want to see European culture ignore it. That's the ambivalence.

I'll never forget that story of the concentration camp guard at Auschwitz doing his German exams on 'Goethe and Humanism', and actually writing his essay and asking some of the Jews in the camp to help him. What a subject to ask someone who, the next day, you are sending to his death. Human beings are quite capable of integrating culture into their barbarism.

GF: *Isn't that taking an unduly cynical view of it?*

DP: It's not cynical. It's a warning note about the too easy assumption that culture ennobles. When people tell me that culture ennobles, I think, hmm, maybe.

GF: *When the* Pennies from Heaven *film was being made you spent a lot of time in Los Angeles. Did you actually live there?*

DP: No. The longest I was ever there was ten days. I would go over for five days, seven days, whatever. It wasn't possible to stay longer because of my health – I have my ointments, dressings, drugs and so on – and also I didn't want to. I would stay in the Beverly Hills Hotel or the Beverly Wilshire, and I thought, 'If I turn up Rodeo Drive once more, I'm going to be ill.' So I travelled back and forth.

GF: *I believe you rewrote* Pennies from Heaven *about twelve times before they decided to do it.*

DP: Oh God, yes, but that's average on an American script. You respond continually to Demand A, Demand B, Demand C, without quite knowing where they're coming from. It could be from an actor, a director, a production designer, it could be the studio – you just don't know. I never actually wrote while I was there. I'd go, I'd talk, I'd recede before it became a problem, and then understand or pretend to understand what they wanted. It was important for me to do that partly because it was American culture, and therefore I was tapping some part of my own mind; but I also sensed things were changing in England, and I needed to get some American dosh into my hands, to make sure I had more manoeuvrability than I otherwise would.

GF: *Did you see the need for some kind of creative autonomy?*

DP: In that craven English way, working in Hollywood automatically improves your status in England. But whatever else happens you do get your hands on more money in Hollywood if you tend not to say, 'No, I won't do this; no, I won't do that.' Poor T. S. Eliot had to go and work in the bank. I regarded going to America as working in the bank – but I was on the right side of the counter.

GF: *What were you trying to achieve with the film of* Pennies from Heaven *that was different from the series? What were your motives for doing it?*

DP: I'm not entirely sure, to be honest. There is a sense in which I wanted to take the musical back to its origins, i.e. the American musical, because that is what is in Arthur's head. He had that English thing of wanting to get to Chicago, and there's the way he uses the word 'Chicago', almost like a touchstone. What worked in the MGM film of *Pennies* were the musical numbers. You had these huge production numbers and some of them were terrific. But they failed to understand that it was supposed to be a *home-made* musical.

When I went to visit the studio I was shown the schoolroom set for the 'Love is Good for Anything That Ails You' number – a simulation of a genuine rural Illinois schoolroom of the thirties – and I thought it was great. Then they said, 'Now we'll show you the fantasy schoolroom,' which was this much bigger, all-white duplication of it. That was the moment I realized they were never going to make it work, but there was no way that that could be conveyed. The whole thing was running, the

28  *Pennies from Heaven*: Steve Martin as Arthur Parker
29  *Pennies from Heaven*: Christopher Walken in the 'Let's
Misbehave' number

cake was baked, and it was eating itself. I'll never allow that to happen to me again. But I didn't know at the time that it was going to happen.

And although, for example, the bar scene, the male stripper number, 'Let's Misbehave', is terrific in the film, the story itself is a stripped-down, soulless précis of what was actually going on. And the very brilliance of the musical numbers destroyed the reason for their being there. They didn't come out of the characters, they didn't come out of the *head*. In the *Pennies* series, even if the dialogue had remained the same, if the actors had sung the songs the whole thing would have collapsed. In effect, that's what happened with the film. Obviously it had lots of remnants of the original in it, and many good things about it, but conceptually it fell by the wayside. The discipline wasn't there. It showed at the test screenings in Denver, where a lot of people walked out. A lot of cuts were made after that.

GF: *Do you think MGM simply didn't understand what you were trying to do?*
DP: They probably didn't. I thought during the preliminary conversations that they did, from the way they responded to the original material. It was partly the cultural gap in understanding – the English use of ironies in speech and so on. I should have been more explicit, more forthright, when I talked to Herb Ross and the MGM people. I should have made sure that they understood the original series better than they appeared to. But being explicit is the very thing I hate doing before I begin writing. So there was this dilemma. And when you go out very late in the shoot and they show you what they've been working on all that time, one doesn't have the brutality to say, 'No, I don't like it.' So I only told them about the things I did like, and left the rest unsaid. The *Singing Detective* script is written in such a way that it won't allow that kind of mistake to be made, if the film gets made. First of all, it's not in any sense like a précis of the original series, and secondly, it is totally re-thought.

GF: *Do you mean you've left no room for misunderstanding the intention behind the songs in your script?*
DP: Yes. It's inescapable. Because *Pennies* is so much simpler it was easy for them to think, 'Ah, a production number, dialogue, story, a little bit of this, a little bit of that, another production number' – and that's the way they did think. And all the American skills in design and so on came out there – in just the wrong places, over the top of it.

Again, that's why, in my opinion, *Cop Rock* doesn't work. It's that

very subtle distinction between using the music in one particular and
fertile way with all its resonances, and using it as something added on.
That's what the MGM *Pennies* became – a series of production numbers
that made little connection with the characters.

GF: *Before Herb Ross directed the film of* Pennies *I believe you'd been
involved with him on another project called* Unexpected Valleys.
DP: It was about a ballet dancer. Herb Ross had been a dancer and his
late wife, Nora Kaye, had been a great American ballerina. He asked to
see me when he was finishing *Nijinsky* at Pinewood. He'd already done
*The Turning Point* and he wanted another script about a female dancer
and the physical effort of ballet. I thought *Unexpected Valleys* was going
to go ahead with Sherry Lansing at 20th Century-Fox. Like many of
these things, it seemed to be on the brink of getting made. God knows,
one's first lesson is that liking the script and getting into all of those
energetic discussions, and doing a rewrite and another draft, and so on,
doesn't necessarily bring you to the green light. But as a result of that
script he got to see an episode or two from the *Pennies from Heaven*
serial and then he asked me to write the *Pennies* script.
    My writing something and then rewriting it like that happened many
times and was a profitable thing to do. It was a source of freedom and
technique, and also helped me realize the two cultures were very different
and that the cosy television culture, which had in a sense nurtured me,
didn't apply out there. There were always projects that fell down at the
last minute and things that happened to the endless drafts of *Pennies*, all
of which compromised what I started out with, but that was the system,
and that's what I received the cheques for. The knowledge, the widening,
the breaking up of some of my insularity was extremely good, if sometimes painful.

GF: *What happened with the plan to do* Double Dare *as a film in
America?*
DP: In that period while *Pennies* was being made, and they thought it
was going to be a great success and I knew it *wasn't* going to be
(although you can never say that; you just introduce an element of cau-
tion wherever possible), they started trawling through all my old work.
They must have thought, 'Oh God, we've got this guy who's written all
these plays.' 'This is the wave of the future,' is what Herb Ross said.
You're not immune to that kind of flattery and you're also not immune to
the large sums being discussed.

So *Double Dare* was a script that I wrote during that period. It was about an English writer who arrives in Hollywood and has 'double' experiences, the same as the character in the BBC play but transplanted, transposed, and even more distant from his roots, his feelings. Hence the alienation in it is much stronger. There is greater sexual fear, banked up with cultural fear, as well as the sense of selling out. The dislocation of place and time in his mind in the nowhere city of Los Angeles is very much part of it.

I am currently having meetings about *Mesmer*, which I wrote nine years ago. Suddenly somebody is interested in making it. The same may well be true of *Double Dare* one day, and of the other scripts I wrote. You never quite know.

GF: *So* Double Dare *could surface yet?*

DP: Yes, it could indeed. I rather hope it does. I think it's interesting, although the script's very menacing and dangerous and *very* sexually disturbing. There's a lot of apprehension and a feeling of dislocation and angst, as well as the sexual anxiety and identity problem of the original play.

GF: *Did you feel that the* Brimstone and Treacle *film was less successful than the play?*

DP: The film was definitely less successful than the play, as often happens.

GF: *Were there compromises?*

DP: Yes, to get it made. I still haven't got any money from that. We made naïve assumptions that it was possible to make the film at a certain price. American money came in. Hence, Sting came in. Hence, I accepted deferments, and then found on the cost statements that there were incidental expenses for things like distribution in South America. I didn't even take first position on the videocassette, which was ignorance. It led to a realization of exactly what it is like out there in the film business.

GF: *What went wrong with* Gorky Park?

DP: Lots of things, but it wouldn't be right to point the finger at anybody. To start with, it is an extremely complex story in detective terms. The fact that it was shot in Helsinki didn't help, but it was then politically impossible to do it in the Soviet Union itself. Also, there was a weird, dangerous mix of acting styles. William Hurt's Method style is

30   *Gorky Park*: William Hurt

almost diametrically opposed to that of those very able British character actors. The film was also severely cut, which only added to the apparent complications of it.

Also, it didn't really have any political footing. Between the delivery of, say, the first draft and whatever draft you're trying to write next – that constant patch-and-mend process – you can easily lose sight of what you're attempting to do, what it was for, what it was about. It's amazing how often that happens in movies with all that money, all that professionalism, all that undoubted skill. On *Gorky Park*, despite the decisions that had already been made, they would gradually change this scene, that scene. Although each change might be justified in itself, the cumulative effect was to shift the axis of the reason for doing it in the first place. It's very characteristic of Hollywood that they buy what they want and then change it into its very opposite.

GF: *After the three filmed plays for LWT you had nothing on television in Britain until 1985. Do you now regard that as a fallow period?*

DP: In one sense it was a holiday. I also had the feeling that I had to step back. I'd had my first taste of how things were going to go with LWT. That was supposed to be a nine-play project, six by me and three by others. They took the three by the others because it was franchise time, and then suddenly found that, after the first one, which was by Jim Allen, there were all sorts of impossibilities, and the contract was terminated. That was a good enough warning of what it was going to be like, in my opinion anyway. I had a growing sense of compromise – signs that less demanding plays would be done. There was a greater emphasis upon series, upon co-production money, universal saleability and so on. And I thought, 'Well, I had better start protecting myself. I had better start being able to say no, so I can earn elsewhere.' This was a sort of lesson not to be too intellectual, but instead to tune into another part of whatever it is that I do, the part that believes in a common culture. But working in America also gave me the tactical advantage of being able to manoeuvre and manipulate myself here. If you live and work in so-called popular culture, even if you're on the extreme edge of it, the one thing you've got to do is keep your wits about you, because that's part of the price of being there. And part of that I quite enjoy, because it tells me what it's really about. So in trying to make the kinds of plays and films you want to make you can either be aggressive, and be accused of that, or you can be cringing. Maybe once or twice I've been combative, but I've certainly been aware of being manipulative with some of those executive people, who can't write, can't direct, can't act, can't sing, can't dance, can't write music, and sit across their desks and tell you that what you want to do isn't possible. Well, my first instinct is to put two fingers up – if I physically *could* put two fingers up! – but my other, more healthy, instinct is to out-manipulate them.

GF: *This suggests an impatience with the corporate mentality of the money men.*

DP: Well, they're different. The essential message is, *they don't know*, and you think, rightly or wrongly, that you *do* know. And even if you're wrong you still know better than they do. It's that classic *Singing Detective* thing – even if you're wrong, you're right. You go, 'Am I right, or am I right?'

GF: *Did going to America give you the muscle you needed to get certain projects made at home?*

DP: Yes, to a degree it did. It gave me more freedom. It also gave me a different grammar. It made me open my very reclusive, narrow, insular head to what had been as a dream to me – the films I had seen as a child, the songs I still listened to. When I worked in America, there it all was, but stripped of its fantasy, naked in front of me, because I could see the source of it. Instead of fantasizing about it, it was very easy then to see, say, how gruelling, how brutal, the pre-production of *The Wizard of Oz* must have been. For example, there's a scene before Dorothy's return home that's completely lost. I have the original soundtrack, and there are a couple of references in the dialogue to a non-existent scene. This happens all the time, and with today's word processors it happens more and more. It's like stumbling upon an old bomb in a field. You know, 'Oh God, there's a body of a previous writer.'

GF: *Has that ever happened to you?*

DP: No, not yet.

GF: *What prompted you to go back to the Revd Dodgson with* Dreamchild *– apart from the fact that Jim Henson's animatronic puppets were bound to be more convincing than the BBC's in* Alice *in 1965?*

DP: I read a paragraph somewhere – I don't know where – which said that Alice Liddell went to New York when she was in her eighties. I said, 'Jesus Christ.' A couple of days later I was writing it. And, as I say, I was done with it in four and a half days.

31   *The Wizard of Oz* (1939)

32  *Dreamchild*: Alice (Amelia Shankley) with the Gryphon and the
Mock Turtle
33  *Dreamchild*: Mrs Hargreaves (Coral Browne) with the Gryphon
and the Mock Turtle

GF: *The flashbacks depict essentially the same story as in* Alice, *except you wrapped round it this extraordinary story of the dowager Alice – Mrs Hargreaves – experiencing culture shock in New York City. It's* Alice in Wonderland *all over again.*

DP: Actually she went with her son, whom I then discovered was quite a fascist, who said, 'One of the problems with America is democracy.' I was interested in the fictive Alice, but I was also interested in the troubled Dodgson character – the fact that Alice's mother tore up his letters. That haunted soul, who didn't stutter when talking to little girls but was done for as soon as they reached puberty . . .

GF: *He seemed to share with John Ruskin and J. M. Barrie that Victorian/Edwardian worship of childhood beauty and innocence.*

DP: Yes, which is interrelated with darker things that one doesn't have to hold in close focus. But we're more aware of it because we know more than they did about sexuality and its repressions, and its convoluted, snake-like approach to emotional release. The idea of that tied-in, repressed, strange, playful, tormented, yet joyously inventive man, and an old woman thinking back because of the culture shock of arriving in New York at that time – that was the engine that started running.

I said to myself, 'How am I going to reach an examination of the anxieties that trouble her? How am I going to approach that theme through her?' I finally realized where it was leading – to the speech she gives at the end. But I didn't start with that. I didn't know how it was going to discharge itself, the buried emotion and regret. And I would have hoped it could have been discharged in a less formal manner. But the shape seemed right, so I left it.

GF: *You make constant references to fairy-tales and children's stories –* Alice in Wonderland, The Wizard of Oz, Rapunzel *– throughout your writing.*

DP: Maybe. I don't know. Perhaps I do.

GF: *For example, in* Christabel, *your 'Alice' is an Englishwoman stranded in Nazi Germany.*

DP: I made her read *Alice in Wonderland*, briefly, that's true. I suspect a lot of that is latent. She's reading to her children, so I think, 'Well, *what* is she reading? – Oh, God. Well, I know *Alice* so I'll put that in.' So it's partly that, but these things fit, you see.

34   *Dreamchild*: producer Kenith Trodd and director Gavin Millar
35   *Dreamchild*: shooting the Mad Hatter's tea party

GF: *I know you were very pleased with* Dreamchild, *which came at a time when the single play was virtually finished in British television.*

DP: Yes, there were a lot of changes afoot that led to changes within me. A lot of my early plays were the old electronic studio plays that you recorded in two days, much more like theatre than film, with four great trundling cameras. Then there was the change, gradually, to using filmed inserts, and then to shooting on film exclusively and in colour, and the peeling-away of the single dramas, from the Wednesday Play to Play for Today. They became less and less popular as American series started coming in and the soaps started. The form of television began to change, as did people's perceptions about it. You shouldn't talk about television in this way, but to use a convenient shorthand it was as though, unconsciously, television were seeking its difference from theatre and film. And the only way that it could really do that was in the serial form. In order to stay one step ahead, which I have always tried to do in television, the single play, as they still called it then (they don't use that word at all now), was no longer an idea that filled my mind. From *Pennies from Heaven* onwards I thought in terms of the bigger unit – because you couldn't show that in cinema. With six or seven episodes you could grab and maybe hold people. But you could also explore your characters with the same density as a novel, if you had, say, seven hours to play with. *Pennies* was longer than that. *The Singing Detective* was longer than that. You've got that unit of time to split. I'd love each episode to go out boom-boom-boom, one after the other, in the same evening. But that's Cloud Cuckoo Land. Where it was most needed was in *Blackeyes*. That should have gone out as one piece; then it would have seemed much less complicated. It sank into its own complications like someone drowning in a bog! But that form interests me more than just a single slot on television.

GF: *There was something about the immediacy of the old electronic studio – a visual clarity – that is lost on film.*

DP: It can be lost on film. On the other hand the electronic studio can lead you to wordiness and towards the non-visual, so there is a plus and a minus either way. Film does lose something on television. The projection beam is coming the wrong way – your eye is the screen and the light comes to your eye, not the other way round. This can add enormously to the intensity of the experience, but it's not the same as the darkened theatre with its audience. All audiences, I've said before, are conspiracies. They join together, in an odd way. They share collectively. Within those four walls they laugh at the same time – or some do, and the others *then* do, which makes them like a club. When actors say, 'What sort of audience is it tonight?' they don't mean how many. They mean something about the *nature* of that collective beast which is the audience.

Television doesn't have that. When you watch television you don't dress up for it, you don't go out for it, you don't pay for it, the lights are on, and you do things and you talk, and all that is largely to the detriment of the experience – but if something is working it can be extraordinarily powerful because it sits right in the middle of that mundaneness.

GF: *Going back to your films,* Track 29, *directed by Nicolas Roeg, uses very similar characters, some dialogue, and many of the situations that you used in* Schmoedipus. *Do you consider it 'based' on that play?*

DP: 'Based on' is wrong. That group of plays in the early seventies had the same kind of obsession: basically, that there's somebody outside the house who's going to knock, and you draw him in, but really he's inside your head. I probably return to that theme again and again. Yes, there are elements I resurrected, but I think any writer really has a very small field to keep ploughing, and eventually you turn up the coins or the treasure or whatever it is you want. I know I always go back to the same motifs, if that's not too grand a word.

Of course *Schmoedipus* was set in England. *Track 29* is set in America and it's more real. *Schmoedipus* was lighter, more satirical. *Track 29* is more the gathering together of anxiety and making it comic, I hope. It's funny, but it's funny-creepy, funny-edgy.

GF: *Gary Oldman's portrayal of Theresa Russell's imaginary son – the return of the repressed – in* Track 29 *was strongly in keeping with Tim Curry's in* Schmoedipus, *but also with Michael Kitchen's in the original* Brimstone *and Tom Bell's in* Angels Are So Few: *the androgynous but sexually threatening boy–man.*

DP: Gary's a formidable actor, and he's almost like a delinquent actor as well. He's on the edge of things. He makes you feel nervous watching him. That quality is innate, I think. I was pleased with his interplay, in particular with Theresa. He is the stranger who's outside but also in your head. He's very much that part of your mind when you're worried and you're not quite going to sleep, when you're not sure whether you're awake or not. I believe he said to Nic at the beginning, 'I don't know what the fuck this is all about.' But I think he knows even when he doesn't know. There are some actors who want to know what the

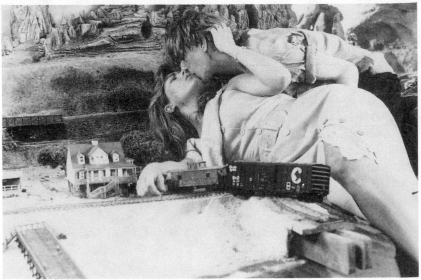

36  *Schmoedipus*: Mother and son? (Anna Cropper and Tim Curry)
37  *Track 29*: Mother and son? (Theresa Russell and Gary Oldman)

character's grandfather had for breakfast, actors who inch towards understanding – I think he gets it all in one go.

GF: *Did you visit the set at all?*
DP: No, because of my health problems. The wind had got into my house again, as it were, and the tiles were falling off me.

GF: *What became of the* Phantom of the Opera *and* Pushkin *film scripts that you had written in the late eighties?*
DP: They dug their own holes. I was really pleased with the *Phantom of the Opera* script. I had changed the setting to Paris in 1940 during the German Occupation, with the Nazis running the opera house. I was playing with the musical genre, the war genre and, obviously, the romance genre. The producers were ecstatic over the first draft and then the second draft, and then they said, 'Now we're going to give it to the director.' And they gave it to a German director who sat down in Claridge's with me and said he found the Germans in it unsympathetic and the writing too melodramatic and clichéd. I remember it was 1 March [1988], and there were a few flurries of snow in the air as I left Claridges'. Suddenly, as I crossed the road through the traffic, I realized I was nearly in tears. And I thought, 'Fuck it, that's it. Let them play. I'm not going to play with them.'

At that time all these things combined to make me say, 'Right, if the producers think a script is a sort of neat, useful accessory for their director to shit upon and scrawl on, without actually sitting down and thinking it through, then there is, indeed, only one place I can go. I will have to start directing them myself.' It was a self-defensive posture. But because I've been at it so long and I believed in what I was doing when I started out, although some of that is eroded, I still retain enough of it to say, 'I've got to protect what I do and keep it going for as long as I can.'

GF: *Among the other scripts you've written that currently seem likely to be produced are* Midnight Movie *and* Mesmer. *What can you say about them?*
DP: The genre that *Midnight Movie* occupies is sort of Hammer horror. It takes a very oblique angle on that and it puts the horrors where they should be! *Mesmer*'s been at the starting gate four times. It's about the late eighteenth-century hypnotist Anton Mesmer, who is half charlatan, half genius. Because the term 'mesmerized' came slightly after him it's both old-fashioned and not quite old-fashioned enough.

# CHAPTER 6

# Director and Novelist

## Blackeyes, Secret Friends

'There's no way you or any other man will ever willingly understand what it is
you make women think of their own bodies.'
Jessica in *Blackeyes* (serial)

In quick succession, between 1988 and 1991, Potter dramatized his two
most recent novels and, never having directed before, directed both of the
new scripts. *Blackeyes*, a novel written in seven weeks and published in
1987, became *Blackeyes* the four-part serial; it was shot on 35 mm. on a
comparatively large BBC budget of £2.4 million in 1989. *Ticket to Ride*,
written in eight weeks between drafts of *The Singing Detective* and published in 1986, became the feature film *Secret Friends* (1992), made for
£1.5 million.

Notwithstanding Potter's illness (his course of drugs staved it off
during the weeks of shooting, enabling him to direct, but causing him to
vomit at the weekends), *Blackeyes* was completed in eighteen weeks, a
marathon stint for any director, let alone a fifty-four-year-old neophyte.
The production, however, was clouded by the on-again, off-again saga of
Potter's stormy relationship with his longtime producer Kenith Trodd,
which had reached an earlier crisis during the making of *The Singing
Detective*. Trodd allegedly walked out on *Blackeyes* just before shooting
began when he learned that Potter would be working with its other
producer, Rick McCallum, on his next serial *Lipstick on your Collar* at
Channel 4.*

None of this could have prepared Potter for the critical and personal

---

* *Lipstick on your Collar* was commissioned by Michael Grade, who in 1980 had
terminated Potter's and Trodd's film deal with LWT. In the event, Potter and McCallum
went their separate ways and Trodd returned to the fold after Potter was told by Channel 4
that he would not be allowed to direct *Lipstick*. Trodd was unable to relaunch the project
with Potter as director at the BBC and it remained at Channel 4 with Renny Rye directing
and Rosemarie Whitman and Potter producing the serial for their company, Whistling
Gypsy, which also produced *Secret Friends* in collaboration with the New York-based
Briarpatch Film Corporation.

abuse volleyed at *Blackeyes* when it was aired on BBC 2 in late 1989. A complex analysis of institutionalized sexism, Potter's serial was condemned for feeding the very sickness it claimed to be diagnosing. The multi-stranded narrative concerns a young woman, Jessica (Carol Royle), whose account of her experiences as a sexually preyed-upon fashion model have become the source of a lascivious best-selling novel by her decrepit windbag uncle, Maurice James Kingsley (Michael Gough). Blackeyes (Gina Bellman), the fictional 'Jessica', is depicted as a beautiful, passive, emotionally void mannequin who drowns herself in the Serpentine with a list of her lovers tucked in her vagina. As Jessica, the police detective investigating the suicide, and her neighbour Jeff (Nigel Planer) – copy-writer, aspiring novelist and putative New Man – seek to reclaim Blackeyes from her watery fate, so reality, perceived reality, fiction and the past (Kingsley molested Jessica as a child) coalesce, and some kind of moral order is restored with Kingsley's violent death and Jessica's liberation. Potter's decision to add a sly, insinuating narration in his own voice only complicated this abstruse but in many ways extremely courageous post-feminist revenge thriller. If Potter made a crucial mistake it was not in showing scenes that were supposed to espouse exploitation, but in not convincing his public that their content was unintended to be titillating to viewers who would elect to see them that way. Significantly, the original novel, dealing with exactly the same themes, had caused barely a ripple of feminist outrage, indicating that the *visual* mediation of Blackeyes's degrading experiences in a television serial was exactly what caused offence – precisely Potter's point in his contention that the objectification of women is damaging to both sexes.

On a likeminded theme, *Secret Friends*, Potter's ensuing project and his first feature as director, also met with disparaging reviews. John (Alan Bates), a middle-aged illustrator of wildflowers, forgets who he is while travelling on a train to London. Once there, he invites a call-girl to his hotel room: the woman who saunters up to his door is the fantasy twin of his wife, Helen (Bellman), who may or may not have worked as a prostitute before she met John. (In this respect, *Secret Friends* echoes the doubling of the actress as a prostitute in a hotel in *Double Dare*.) John, it seems, can make love to Helen only if he imagines her a prostitute. However, his puritanical disgust for her in this role drives him to kill her.

The source of John's inability to relate to women as anything but whores, the splintering of his personality, and even his fastidiousness as an artist are revealed as memories rise up from the unconscious swamp:

John's father was an ascetic country parson who drilled the boy in botanical lore and withheld him from maternal affection this prompted John to invent a profane ally who has stayed on to steer his adult fantasies into the realm of sadomasochism. A secret sharer in John's fantasies, Helen not only projects her own fantasies on to his but imagines that she stabs both Angela (Frances Barber), a family friend John has slept with, and Martin (Tony Doyle), a family friend who calls on her in John's absence. In the end, John is able to banish his secret friend and his corrupting fantasies and he and Helen are reunited, although how he gathers up the shards of his fractured identity is rendered without the logic that attended, say, Marlow's psychological reassemblage in *The Singing Detective*, or, for that matter, Jessica's in *Blackeyes*. Nor does the jaunty comic style of the film sit well with the weft of psychic processes that made the novel *Ticket to Ride* a much more successful endeavour.

GF: *What have you been able to do in your novels that you feel you couldn't do in your plays?*

DP: I would guess not very much. I'm not a novelist. The motive for writing them probably resides elsewhere than in the proper motives of a novelist. They weren't exactly exercises, but it was a return to the source – to what it's like to write prose, which is of course the origin of all writing. There's a certain freedom and relief in writing a sentence and saying, 'He saw,' 'He felt,' 'She felt,' 'She saw,' as opposed to simply writing *what* he said, *what* she said. That's what's valuable to me. I do think my novels are quite well written, but really they are *springs*.

   I think the novel is almost dead. It's a late literary form that rises in the eighteenth century and dies, or nearly dies, in the twentieth century. Why do we use the word 'novel'? It means 'new'. It grew up with the bourgeoisie and it placed a central character in a stable order. Hence, a recent plethora of experimental novels: novels that keep telling you you're reading a novel. That classic question 'Who is writing it?' is crucial. Some novelists write, 'I got up and walked through a door.' But I say, 'Who says so?' Novels survive better in their genre forms, like the detective story or the thriller, but the novel *per se* is in a bit of a crisis.

GF: Hide and Seek, *your first novel, addresses that question of authorship. You have a novelist writing a novel who's contemptuous of his protagonist, but gradually the protagonist (who's called 'Daniel Miller', an approximation of 'Dennis Potter') takes over and terminates the narrative. You traverse some familiar territory in there – the Forest of Dean, illness, male puritan disgust for female sexuality – and there are descriptions or images that you also used in* Angels Are So Few, Follow the Yellow Brick Road *and* The Singing Detective, *but the book is primarily an angry deconstruction of itself, in which you heap scorn on the very structures you use.*

DP: It's a stripping away. Not only am I writing a novel, I am also saying, 'How ridiculous to write a novel.' It's one of the ways of keeping the novel form alive, because it's really embalmed.

GF: *Are there any contemporary novelists that you admire?*

DP: I enjoyed *The Wasp Factory* by Iain Banks because that was occupying a different territory. Martin Amis is very tight, supremely skilled, very funny, and sometimes disturbing. But he's trapped as a novelist. He's like that bit in T. S. Eliot – he does a piece in all these different voices, a complicated perpetual parody. It's funny but it's not real, and you're always aware of that.

GF: *You yourself have used caricature and clichés for different effects in lots of places.*

DP: Yes, but in a different form. I see drama as the oldest form and the one that will always be there, and it's capable of using all those things because of its relationship to an audience, as opposed to a reader. Drama can do it all – it's all in there. Except it can't say, 'Here's a page. Read it.' But then that's asking red to be blue. Drama can address humankind more consistently, with more competence, demonstrably over longer periods of time than 'the novel'. The classical nineteenth-century novels remain as great memorials, but because of the time and distance, because of our knowledge of what has happened, we can read them as *that*, and enter into them in that way. For example, I never thought I would like Trollope's naturalism, but I do now. But whether it's Tolstoy on one level or Trollope on another, with Hardy or Dickens somewhere in between, none of them had doubts about the form. If you sit down to write a novel now, if you've got any intellect or any sensitivity to what forms of communication are today, the form of the novel will trouble you. Whether drama is expressed in the theatre or television or film, or even in a video game, the structure remains drama.

GF: *Why did you write* Blackeyes *as a novel and why did you choose to adapt it for a series?*

DP: The answer to why you write anything is almost always difficult to

38  *Blackeyes*: Gina Bellman

answer. You *find* yourself writing something. That's what it amounts to
in the end. You proceed further and further into a piece of writing. Then
it becomes important to try and finish it, or abandon it.

There was something in the air about feminists and about women as
commodities, most classically expressed, of course, or most easily
expressed if you like, by beautiful young models who are turned into
things, things that are bought, sex. In Marxist terms, it's reification. Sex
is used to sell. But the very manner in which those models are manipulated tells you a great deal about the *whole* of the culture, not just the
sexual culture, but the way men see, men rule. Men are the oldest and the
newest ruling class, in that sense.

And I wanted to find a way of showing that metaphorically, by having
a model who was like the figures you see on the hoardings in posters and
in photos in gossip magazines, but who seldom spoke, seldom acted out
of independent initiative – was, in other words, a creature *made* by that
kind of world, and all the sleaze that draws to it. The novel showed that,
to a degree, but because it was prose I couldn't see it in my head –
because I am not a novelist. I wanted to see it in order to understand it. I
wanted *it* to be seen in order to be understood, put it that way. Which, of
course, in turn dictated, in my head at least, the style in which it should
be done, which is trying to use the camera as the force of alienation itself.
It was at one and the same time prurient and dispassionate. It was trying
to get into the subject *and* prowl round it. It was trying to be objective at
the same time as it was being contaminated. This is also why I added the
narrator's voice – to get to the ambivalence of that, and to show that
when you show exploitation you also exploit.

It was about the terrible ambivalence in the invention of sexual images
to sell. That invention of images is what we do all the time. In *Blackeyes* I
was saying we should beware of the stories we tell of ourselves because
we start to believe in them; they become what we see. We think what we
*think* we think when we make up such stories! I don't mean stories in the
sense of narrative, but the whole signalling mechanism we have in our
culture, central to which are sexual images, which are the most refined,
the most worked-on, and the most overt as well. If there's an image of a
beautiful woman on a hoarding and a man walking along the street sees
it and his eyes alight on it, it potentially corrupts him more than it does
the girl on the poster, but it corrupts and brutalizes both sexes, or can do.
I tried to show this in *Blackeyes*, where I had the old writer using his
niece's memories of being a model for his novel, but within that story had
someone trying to rescue the model. But since he was an inventive person

39  *Blackeyes*: Michael Gough as the novelist Maurice James Kingsley
40  Dennis Potter directing *Blackeyes*

as well, he contributes to that whole interlaying of invention, the invention of sexual image, which dooms the model Blackeyes, unable to articulate anything, right from the word 'Go'. But there were too many strands, and the style, which is very alienating, was so successful it alienated every fucking person who ever saw it!

GF: *A problem with it was that in showing a woman taking control of her life, an idea that on paper should have appealed to the feminist lobby, you also showed, unavoidably, the sexist imagery that had entrapped her.*

DP: She was trying to take control of her life from an impossible position. There was no control that she could exert. That was the point. If it had been written by a woman I think people would have seen that straight away. A lot of them did, of course. But part of the corruption is that you cannot enter into the centre of this and show what's really going on without people saying, 'You are doing exactly the thing that you are attacking.'

GF: *But there is that sexual display of Blackeyes – and of Gina Bellman, the actress who played her – which was inevitably going to make people say, 'This is sexist.'*

DP: Yes, of course they are. But what I was trying to show was that, at the very moment of looking at this beautiful girl who has nothing on and is passively accepting a sexual onslaught, you are being pulled in. The very thing that feminists rightly object to – those hoardings, soft porn and so on – was being used to take you into it and *then* to make you feel the alienation, to show how *dead* that world is, how manipulative those things are, how they betray the manipulator as well as the manipulated. There was no other route into that. It's a time bomb. You hurt yourself when you do it.

GF: *You did the voice-over yourself. Was that admitting your own culpability?*

DP: In a way. Right from the very beginning the voice-over put that right up front. But it was also another character and a last-minute, desperate attempt to pull all these strands together. Not only were you showing the manipulation within the story, you had this manipulator *narrating* it. I was hoping that out of that collision, that multiplicity of exploitation and manipulation being demonstrated in an almost explicitly Brechtian way, you would feel the alienation. The idea was to live within it instead of illustrating it. Instead of just moralizing and saying, 'Here is A, and A is bad, isn't it? and I am B, telling you that A is bad,' I wanted A and B to corrupt each other. That was the dramatic method.

I think one day people will see it. I hope so. But of course one of the things that happened was that *Blackeyes* released a tide of polemical abuse of such huge proportions in the English tabloids that it was almost proof that I was stepping on the right nerves, if not in totally the right way. Some of those middle-aged TV critics in the tabloids were *screaming*. So something was clearly going on; quite what, we have yet to see.

GF: *You had been charged with misogyny before* Blackeyes. *Male characters in many of your earlier works seethe with puritanical disgust for women they sexually desire; they pour out torrents of invective against them.*

DP: They blame women because that's the source of their unease and their wistfulness and their sexual tension. That's traditional male language. You blame it on the temptress, in religious culture the unclean vessel. But of course it's coming from the man.

GF: *It's transferred self-disgust, the result of frustration due to an inability to possess these women.*

DP: Yes, all that. Women are turned into property, consumer objects for just that reason. Men feel they must *own* women in that way.

GF: *Do you think the accusations of misogyny against you have ever been justified?*

DP: In some part they may be justified. If you come up with English working-class male ideas about women, then traces of that – no, more than traces – a lot of that is going to cling to you for a long time.

GF: *In terms of the writing, what was the evolution of the* Blackeyes *series and the unreleased movie version?*

DP: I wrote the film using no new material, or so I thought. But inevitably I found that I wanted to change everything, so I had to go back and rewrite the original four parts. I found there was a relationship between the four- and the one-part versions in the narrative styles that fascinated me. And then I thought, 'I can't bear to hand this over to anybody.'

GF: *Because people failed to understand what you were attempting in* Blackeyes, *did you feel you had failed?*

DP: I did fail. If there's such universal rejection and opposition and incomprehension then it's extremely likely that it was either badly written, or badly done, or both.

GF: *Given its contentious subject, it was a risky project with which to make your début as a director.*

DP: It was. I had asked others to do it earlier. Nicolas Roeg was on the brink of doing it, and then said no he wouldn't. Finally I couldn't ask anyone. I knew what kind of risk I was taking, what kind of journey I was *trying* to make, and I approached it in a spirit of melancholy resolve. I had the opportunity to do it – I was *placed* to do it. I did feel rather melancholy about killing off my old self. Taking Methotrexate meant I would be able to direct in the week but would then vomit at the weekends. When I explained about my health to Mark Shivas, the head of film at the BBC, when they were taking out all this completion insurance on me, he said, 'You won't be vomiting only at the weekends, you'll be doing it every morning as well!' I didn't approach it in a chirpy way. I had to stop writing for a year and I had to crack the shell of my reclusiveness, my working habits, my medication habits, but I felt there was nowhere else for me to go. I felt compelled, in a way, and I felt that I would do it properly. That's all I can say.

Maybe I wasted the chances, and you really only get one – except I got two. I did the same thing on *Secret Friends*. I appointed another director on that at first, but he wasn't accepted. I wanted to get it made and I thought, 'Well, I am going to be asking the same things of someone on *Secret Friends* that I would have asked them on *Blackeyes*, things I shouldn't be asking other people to do.' Because they both involved such complicated narratives, and because both occupied the same ground, although in slightly different ways, they needed a kind of suicidal commitment to them. If I had started with a straight linear narrative I could probably now pick and choose what I wanted to direct next, but I can't. That's the price you pay – that's the way of the world when you get so many chances. So that's it – I've had it!

GF: *Were you personally satisfied with your direction of* Blackeyes *and* Secret Friends?

DP: I would only claim this: that there was something interesting going on. And that something cannot at this moment be seen through the narrative nature of those films – *non*-narrative nature is a better description of it. What is going on, filmically, will be worth looking at again

41   Dennis Potter directing Alan Bates in *Secret Friends*

42 *Secret Friends*: Alan Bates
43 *Secret Friends*: Gina Bellman

when some of this is past. That's all I will say, which implies, of course, that the answer to your question is yes. Oh God! It also implies I don't want to answer your question.

GF: *How much of the fragmented consciousness of the Alan Bates character, John, in* Secret Friends *was in the script and how much was worked out in the cutting room?*

DP: A lot of it was in the script and a lot in the cutting room. I think the cutting room is like writing. I love the cutting room. Because I didn't want there to be a difference between fantasy and reality, there was a recognition that, 'Oh God, the narrative line is going to be really confusing.' So you try many ways of not capturing, but illustrating – not even illustrating but *living within* what he was going through in his head. The basic decision in the cutting room was to keep the stuff on the railway train as the only 'present tense', so you can see his journey, as it were. That may have been a mistake, but that's one of the wonderful things about being in a cutting room. You can make those mistakes – if they are mistakes. The film was a continual collision of fantasy and reality, so it was always going to be difficult.

GF: *Repressed from childhood, John can only make love to his wife if she behaves like a prostitute, and eventually she starts to believe she is one. As with* Blackeyes, *isn't* Secret Friends *showing how that semi-pornographic lexicon of lipstick and high-heels and so on can be corrupting?*

DP: Yes, it's dealing with the commerciality of sex, if you like, because that's the most extreme expression of it. But it's the reactions of that extremity that are interesting to me. There is the beautiful and purchasable woman, there is the man capable of thinking of sex as a commodity and as a commercial transaction, and their real feelings get tangled up in it – but sex is not a commodity. The fantasy and the lust gets transferred to other people and other things, and then turns in like a knife on itself.

GF: *Your films and plays often present this tormenting, quasi-religious, and ultimately misogynistic notion of women as both angels and whores. Do you think that male dichotomy is something that can be resolved – are the two things reconcilable?*

DP: No. The two images are ludicrously far apart and they should both be destroyed. The whore–angel, being momentarily one and then the other, is interesting, but it's not valid either. By putting the two together and examining the collisions between the two you can start working out what cannot be worked out in the existence of physical desire and the existence of love. Desire uses the language of love, and love is fuelled, obviously, by the flow of desire. And because desire is universal and love is particular you are going to get an enormous tangle of feelings. But there is no prescription you can write; it's a fact that exists, and it's true of human relationships, which have to contend with both our animality and our grace.

Desires and emotions are cousins to each other to such an extent that sometimes you don't know which is which, and in human relationships tenderness will creep in, or violence will creep in, or self-hatred will creep in, or puritanism. But they will all be trembling on the edge of the same brink, which it's only possible to describe in fiction or poetry, or music. It's like trying to describe the fear of death, which is universal. It's like trying to describe joy, which is also universal.

# CHAPTER 7

# Conclusion

HOPPER: You just got to look around, entcha? I mean, you can't put your
finger on it, but – it's there, definitely there.

FRANCIS: What is?

HOPPER: Change.

*Lipstick on your Collar*

GF: *Given the unfavourable reception of both* Blackeyes *and* Secret
Friends, *how do you now regard your experience as a director and how
does it relate to your future plans?*

DP: I suspect nobody now would fund something that I was directing. I
also paid an enormous price physically for doing it, keeping going with a
mixture of sleeping tablets and alcohol and sometimes vomiting on the
set. Each weekend, when you're supposed to rest, I didn't have any rest,
simply because of the demands of having to take Methotrexate.

I don't know whether I could come to that starting gate again with
anything like the optimism, having had the disappointment and some
disillusion, but also the knowledge that maybe I shouldn't, maybe I need
a mediator. Part of the reason for doing it, I suppose, was also the
knowledge that a film is *written* first. It can continue to be written in that
enormous collaborative act that comes from everyone during production.
But the contribution of the writer has been, is being, and will be continually downgraded, which means you get films that have less and less
content.

Just as in television I had wanted to do something about that, I wanted
to do something about it in film – 'do something about it' sounds too
grandiose, but I was unconscious of that fact anyway. One of the ways I
can still express that is by taking more control, not in order to say to
people, 'You can't change this and you can't do that,' but to make the
thing retain the coherence that it has when the empty page is gradually
being filled up. One of the ways I may be able to do this, which is why I
did *Lipstick on your Collar* this way, is to be a producer in the proper

sense of the word, involved with everything, and all those millions of little, so-called 'artistic' decisions. That will probably better fulfil my needs, in terms of my health and energy, but also in terms of my experience, and also in terms of whatever clout I've got left, which I think will be enhanced again when *Lipstick* comes out. So I will, I hope, be back in the situation I was at the time of *The Singing Detective*, say.

GF: *What are your feelings about the ongoing upheavals in British television?*
DP: I don't have any, really. I know they're going to cock it up. The people who worry about those sorts of things are the people who worry about money and organization, and they don't worry about programmes, they don't worry about the content of programmes. I shall just keep trying to do what I am trying to do. If they make it impossible there's nothing I can do about it. I regard the Rupert Murdochs of this world with maximum contempt anyway, and I'm not even going to enter their terms of argument.

GF: *As you go on, do you see your interests, your concerns, shifting or hardening?*
DP: I don't know, and I'm glad I don't know. Just in terms of work, I am going to roll on, I hope.

GF: *Do you think you are more optimistic now than when you started?*
DP: If I have to enter into that dualism between optimism and pessimism, I just don't know how to reply. I don't feel pessimistic, put it that way. People who are up against it in any sort of shape or form – whether it's in political crisis, war, health, bereavement, domestic crisis, whatever – are far more resilient than they ever bargained on being. That's because there is a tremendous appetite in human beings to live through the most extreme and cruel circumstances. It's shown again and again that the business of life is living, to attend to what it is to live.

GF: *Do you want to write until you can't write any more?*
DP: I think I'm already at that stage, don't you? I'm about there. It's my job – that's all I can say. I can't imagine what I'd do if I didn't. Writing and what you have to attend to after, like producing – in the way that I believe a producer should be like: getting a thing going and then nourishing and cosseting it, bringing out from it what is in it, with all of those people that surround you, and all of *their* people and all of *their* skills.

Without that I wouldn't know what to do. There'd be no point. Yes, I will write until something knocks down my hand, I suppose. What that something might be I am not willing to contemplate!

GF: *Do you still get pleasure out of the writing process?*
DP: Yes, I do. I cuss it as well. Writing is difficult and directing is difficult, but then anything is difficult – playing a good game of football is difficult, isn't it?

GF: *Is there a piece you favour among your plays, film and series, that you feel has been most successful in achieving what you wanted to achieve?*
DP: No, but there are different aspects of different plays that pleased me. *Blue Remembered Hills*, in dealing with its own set of problems, was satisfying to pull off. In terms of lucidity of a difficult argument – argument is not quite the correct word, but I am using it for shorthand – it would be *Where Adam Stood*. In terms of satisfaction with the emotional resonance and depth of a piece, it would be *The Singing Detective*. And in terms of fun, the *Pennies from Heaven* series – and now, much more than either of the previous two legs of this trilogy, *Pennies from Heaven* and *The Singing Detective*, it would be *Lipstick on your Collar*. I think *Lipstick* is the one that people are going to approach more easily and enjoy more readily than most of my other stuff. That might be a good sign, mightn't it?

GF: *How do you think you've managed to be so prolific over the years?*
DP: By working hard. When I lost my job on the *Daily Herald*, and I had three small kids and could scarcely move and things like that, I didn't know what the hell I would do. I measured then, quite directly, my own dignity in terms of whether I could keep my family. But out of that I discovered, in a sense, what it was like to have a vocation – to use a really antique word. So I have always sat down and written, although I tear up more than I finish. And I made it an obligation to myself – to that other part of myself – a duty, if you like, to whatever it was that was given to me, to make sure that I don't waste it. So I work.

GF: *Is writing still a vocation for you?*
DP: I suppose it must be, yes.

# Filmography

TELEVISION

Dennis Potter is writer on all titles. Dates refer to original broadcast dates in Britain.

## 1965

### The Confidence Course
A BBC Television production for The Wednesday Play series
BBC 1, 24 February
*Producer*: James MacTaggart
*Director*: Gilchrist Calder
*Story editor*: Roger Smith
*Designer*: Lionel Radford
*Cast*: Dennis Price (*The Director*), Neil McCarthy (*Black*), Artro Morris (*Jones*), John Moore (*Thomas*), Stanley Baxter (*Hazlitt*), William Moore (*Hammond*), Yootha Joyce (*Rosalind Arnold*), John Quentin (*Broom*), John Blythe (*Greenway*), Joan Sanderson (*Mrs Walker*), Olive Kirby (*Miss Ellwood*), Geoffrey Matthews (*narrator, voice only*)
75 minutes, black and white

### Alice
A BBC Television production for The Wednesday Play series
BBC 1, 13 October
*Producer*: James MacTaggart
*Director*: Gareth Davies
*Film cameraman*: Charles Parnall
*Designer*: Michael Wield
*Film editor*: Peter Pierce
*Cast*: George Baker (*Revd Charles L. Dodgson*), Deborah Watling (*Alice Liddell*), Rosalie Crutchley (*Mrs Liddell*), David Langton (*Dean Liddell*), Tessa Wyatt (*Lorina Liddell*), Maria Coyne (*Edith Liddell*), Malcolm Webster (*Revd R. Duckworth*), Maurice Hedley (*Alexander MacMillan*), John Moffatt (*Mr Stotman*), Peter Bartlett (*Dormouse*), John Bailey (*Mad Hatter*), John Saunders (*March Hare*), Keith Campbell (*Caterpillar*), Norman Scace (*Mock Turtle*), Frank Shelley (*Gryphon*), Billy Russell (*gardener*)
75 minutes, black and white

### Stand Up, Nigel Barton
A BBC Television production for The Wednesday Play series
BBC 1, 8 December

*Producer*: James MacTaggart
*Director*: Gareth Davies
*Story editor*: Tony Garnett
*Telerecording engineer*: Paddy Wilson
*Designer*: Richard Henry
*Cast*: Keith Barron (*Nigel Barton*), Jack Woolgar (*Harry Barton*), Barbara Keogh (*Mrs Taylor*), Janet Henfrey (*Miss Tillings*), Terence Soall (*scout*), Johnny Wade (*Georgie*), Godfrey James (*Bert*), Vickery Turner (*Jill*), Charles Collingwood (*Tim*), Robert Mill (*Adrian*), Katherine Parr (*Mrs Barton*), Charles Lewsen (*president of the union*), Peter Madden (*Jordan*), Alan Lake (*Arthur*), Brian Hankins (*Conrad*), Edward Palmer (*Ernie*)
75 minutes, black and white

## Vote, Vote, Vote for Nigel Barton

A BBC Television production for The Wednesday Play series
BBC 1, 15 December
*Producer*: James MacTaggart
*Director*: Gareth Davies
*Story editors*: Roger Smith, Tony Garnett
*Film cameraman*: James Balfour
*Designer*: Julia Trevelyan Oman
*Film editor*: Bill Brind
*Telerecording editor*: Julian Farr
*Cast*: Keith Barron (*Nigel Barton*), Valerie Gearon (*Anne Barton*), John Bailey (*Jack Hay*), Cyril Luckham (*Archibald-Lake*), Barbara Atkinson (*first hunting woman*), Agatha Carroll (*second hunting woman*), Donald Hewlett (*hunting man*), Russell Forehead (*Sir Harry Blakerswood*), Huw Thomas (*newsreader*), Betty Bowden (*Lady Chairman*), Margaret Diamond (*Lady Secretary*), Madge Brindley (*Mrs Thompson*), Michael Segal (*first questioner*), Raymond Witch (*second questioner*), Charles Rea (*pedestrian*), Dorothea Rundle (*woman*), Sonia Graham (*Mrs Phillips*), Aimée Delamain (*Mrs Morris*), Walter Hall (*Mr Smith*), Keith Campbell (*male nurse*), Harold Bennett (*old man*), Edmund Bailey (*Eddie*), George Desmond (*Mr Harrison*), Fred Berman (*toastmaster*), John Evitts (*journalist*), Alan Laurence (*fat man*), Arthur Ridley (*mayor*)
80 minutes, black and white

## 1966

## Emergency – Ward 9

A BBC Television production for the Thirty-Minute Theatre series
BBC 2, 11 April
*Producer*: Harry Moore
*Director*: Gareth Davies
*Story editor*: Kenith Trodd
*Designer*: Paul Allen
*Cast*: Terence De Marney (*Flanders*), Tenniel Evans (*Padstow*), Dan Jackson (*Adzola*), Gillian Lewis (*Angela*), Paul Carson (*first doctor*), Anwer Begg (*second doctor*), Rowena Gregson (*night nurse*), Evangeline Banks (*sister*), Raymond Witch (*Mr Vyshinski*), John T. Moore (*old man*), Philip Needs (*youth*), Sheelagh McGrath (*nurse*), Dean Anthony (*nurse*)
30 minutes, black and white

## Where the Buffalo Roam
A BBC Television production for The Wednesday Play series
BBC 1, 2 November
*Producer*: Lionel Harris
*Director*: Gareth Davies
*Story editor*: Kenith Trodd
*Designer*: Julian Williams
*Film editor*: Howard Billingham
*Cast*: Hywel Bennett (*Willy*), Megs Jenkins (*Mrs Turner*), Aubrey Richards (*Grandad*), Glyn Houston (*Mr Jenkins*), Richard Davies (*Mr Black*), Denise Buckley (*Susan*), Rhiann John (*Carol*), David Morrell (*Willy's father*), Dilys Davies (*schoolteacher*), Brinley Jenkins (*police superintendent*), Ieuan Rhys Williams (*police inspector*), Kate Jones (*woman in cinema*), Emrys Cleaver (*man in cinema*), Hubert Hughson (*cinema manager*), Ronnie Williams (*newsreader*), D. C. Mills Davies, Dillwyn Owen, Harry Oatten (*policemen*)
75 minutes, black and white

## 1967

## Message for Posterity
A BBC Television production for The Wednesday Play series
BBC 1, 3 May
*Producer*: Lionel Harris
*Director*: Gareth Davies
*Story editor*: Kenith Trodd
*Designer*: John Cooper
*Cast*: Joseph O'Conor (*Sir David Browning*), Patrick Magee (*James Player*), Patricia Lawrence (*Gillian*), Geoffrey Chater (*Richard Browning*), Donald Hewlett (*Hawkins*), Anna Calder-Marshall (*Clara*), Gordon Whiting (*Thompson*), Tony Holland (*Miles*), Keith Campbell (*manservant*), John Golightly (*Karl*)
75 minutes, black and white

## 1968

## The Bonegrinder
A Rediffusion London production for The Playhouse series
ITV, 13 March
*Director*: Joan Kemp-Welch
*Designer*: Fred Pusey
*Film editor*: Mike Taylor
*Cast*: George Baker (*George King*), Margaret Tyzack (*Gladys King*), Weston Gavin (*Sam Adams*)
78 minutes, black and white

## Shaggy Dog
An LWT production for The Company of Five series
ITV, 10 November
*Producer*: Stella Richman
*Director*: Gareth Davies
*Designer*: John Emery

*Cast*: John Neville (*Mr Wilkie*), Ann Bell (*receptionist*), Cyril Luckham (*Mr James*), Ray Smith (*Mr Johnson*), Derek Godfrey (*Mr Parker*), Jane Murdoch (*girl in lift*)
52 minutes, black and white

## A Beast with Two Backs

A BBC Television production for The Wednesday Play series
BBC 1, 20 November
*Producer*: Graeme McDonald
*Director*: Lionel Harris
*Script editors*: Shaun MacLoughlin, Kenith Trodd
*Film cameraman*: Kenneth Westbury
*Film editor*: Howard Kennett
*Designer*: William McCrow
*Cast*: Patrick Barr (*Joe*), Denis Carey (*Ebenezer*), Basil Henson (*the inspector*), Madeleine Newbury (*Joan*), Geraldine Newman (*Rebecca*), Christian Rodska (*Rufus*), Roger Gartland (*Jack*), Terence Sewards (*Will*), Anthony Andrews (*Harry*), Audine Leith (*Nellie*), Laurence Carter (*Micky*), Esther Lawrence (*Mary*), Llewellyn Rees (*Arnold*), Ron Eagleton (*policeman*), Rica Fox (*organist*), Rosalie Horner (*barmaid*), Gina (*Gina, the bear*)
70 minutes, black and white

## 1969

### Moonlight on the Highway

A Kestrel production for LWT's Saturday Night Theatre series
ITV, 12 April
*Producer*: Kenith Trodd
*Director*: James MacTaggart
*Designer*: John Clements
*Cast*: Ian Holm (*David Peters*), Anthony Bate (*Dr Chilton*), Deborah Grant (*Marie Holdsworth*), Robin Wentworth (*Hon. President*), Frederick Peisley (*Gerald*), Wally Patch (*old Londoner*), Arthur Lovegrove (*landlord*), Derek Woodward (*first medical student*), John Flanagan (*second medical student*), Michael Burrell (*barman*)
52 minutes, black and white

### Son of Man

A BBC Television production for The Wednesday Play series
BBC 1, 16 April
*Producer*: Graeme McDonald
*Director*: Gareth Davies
*Story editor*: Shaun MacLoughlin
*Designer*: Spencer Chapman
*Cast*: Colin Blakeley (*Jesus*), Robert Hardy (*Pontius Pilate*), Bernard Hepton (*Caiaphas*), Brian Blessed (*Peter*), Edward Hardwicke (*Judas*), Godfrey Quigley (*Roman commander*), Patricia Lawrence (*Procla*), Gawn Grainger (*Andrew*), Clive Graham (*Roman centurion*), Godfrey James (*1st soldier*), Eric Mason (*2nd soldier*), Brian Spink (*zealot*), Hugh Futcher (*1st heckler*), Raymond Witch (*2nd heckler*), Robin Chadwick (*young officer*), Colin Rix (*James*), Walter Hall (*Philip*), Wendy Allnutt (*Ruth*)
90 minutes, black and white

1970

## Lay Down Your Arms
A Kestrel production for LWT's Saturday Night Theatre series
ITV, 23 May
*Producer*: Kenith Trodd
*Director*: Christopher Morahan
*Designer*: Michael Yates
*Cast*: Nikolas Simmonds (*Private Bob Hawk*), Leonard Trolley (*Lt-Col. Bateman*), Peter Cellier (*Major Hisscock*), John Warner (*Major Wilson*), Graham Armitage (*Major Timps*), Ken Wayne (*Colonel Feather*), James Cairncross (*Julian*), Julia Jones (Mrs Hawk), Joby Blanshard (*Mr Hawk*), George Layton (*Corporal May*), Michael Cashman (*Pete*), Therese McMurray (*Pat*), Tony Caunter (*Mick*), David Webb (*Fred*)
75 minutes, colour

## Angels Are So Few
A BBC Television production for The Wednesday Play series
BBC 1, 5 November
*Producer*: Graeme McDonald
*Director*: Gareth Davies
*Script editor*: Ann Scott
*Film cameraman*: John Turner
*Designer*: Stanley Morris
*Film editor*: Ken Pearce
*Cast*: Tom Bell (*Michael Biddle*), Christine Hargreaves (*Cynthia Nicholls*), Susan Richards (*Mrs Cawser*), Erik Chitty (*Mr Cawser*), Barry Cookson (*Richard Nicholls*), Godfrey James (*postman*), Beryl Cooke (*storyteller*), John Glyn Jones (*clergyman*), Kenneth Ives (*interviewer*), Denise Buckley (*Danish girl*), Dorothea Rundle (*old lady*), Matthew Davies (*Timothy*)
60 minutes, colour

1971

## Paper Roses
A Granada Television production
ITV, 13 June
*Producer*: Kenith Trodd
*Director*: Barry Davis
*Designer*: Alan Price
*Film editor*: Don Kelly
*Cast*: Bill Maynard (*Hubbard*), John Carson (*Joe*), Desmond Penny (*Bladdy*), Donald Gee (*Chart*), William Simons (*Payer*), Aimée Delamain (*Mrs Hubbard*), Joe Gladwin (*messenger*), Rosalie Williams (*neighbour*), Harry Beety (*police sergeant*), Peter Childs (*police constable*), Kim Corlette (*Anne*), Dudley Jones (*the critic*)
55 minutes, black and white

## Traitor
A BBC Television production for the Play for Today series
BBC 1, 14 October
*Producer*: Graeme McDonald

*Director*: Alan Bridges
*Designer*: Tony Abbott
*Script editor*: Ann Scott
*Film editor*: Peter Coulson
*Film cameraman*: Elmer Cossey
*Cast*: John Le Mesurier (*Adrian Harris*), Jack Hedley (*James*), Neil McCallum (*Blake*), Diana Fairfax (*Lady Emma*), Vincent Ball (*Simpson*), Lyndon Brook (*Sir Arthur Harris*), Sean Maddox (*little Adrian*), Jon Laurimore (*Thomas*), John Saunders (*schoolmaster*), Richard Marner (*Michaelov*), Terence Bayler (*duty clerk*), John Quentin (*Craig*)
60 minutes, colour

## Casanova

A BBC Television production
BBC 2, 16 November–21 December
*Producer*: Mark Shivas
*Associate producer*: Fraser Lowden
*Directors*: John Glenister (episodes 1, 2, 4), Mark Cullingham (3, 5, 6)
*Designer*: Peter Seddon
*Videotape editor*: Ron Bowman
*Script editor*: Shaun MacLoughlin
*Film editor*: Graham Bunn
*Film cameramen*: John Wyatt, Ken Westbury, Stewart Farnell
*Cast*: Frank Finlay (*Casanova*), Norman Rossington (*Lorenzo*), Patrick Newell (*Schalon*), David Swift (*Valenglart*), Victor Baring (*Messer Grande*), Christine Noonan (*Barberina*), Zienia Merton (*Christina*), Elaine Donnelly (*Helena*), Julia Cornelius (*Rose*), Brigid Erin Bates (*Manon*), Caroline Dowdeswell (*Anna*), Ania Mason (*Anne Roman-Coupier*), Lyn Yeldham (*Genoveffa*), Rowan Wylie (*Colombina*), Tim Thomas (*Arlecchino*), Basil Clarke (*Dr Bellotti*)
*Episode 1: 'Steed in the Stable' only*: George Benson (*Uncle*), Geoffrey Wincott (*Senator Bragadin*), Christopher Hancock (*Circospetto*), Ronald Adam (*senior inquisitor*)
*Episode 2: 'One at a Time' only*: Arthur Pentelow (*caretaker*), Oliver Butterworth (*concert master*)
*Episode 3: 'Magic Moments' only*: Frederick Peisley (*Capitani*), Hugh Portnow (*Pantalone*), Emil Wolk (*il capitano*), Christopher Martin (*man with knife*)
*Episode 4: 'Window, Window' only*: Jean Holness (*Madame Morin*), Norman Tyrrell (*man in coach*), Simon Barclay (*Damiens*), Richard Dennis (*Tiretta*), Claire Davenport (*Mme Lenoir*), Jo Anderson (*'La Lambertini'*), Sarah Benfield (*Mlle de la Mare*), Enid Burton, Julie Desmond, Sue Bond (*whores*), Norman McGlen (*violinist*)
*Episode 5: 'Fevers of Love' only*: Valerie Gearon (*Pauline*), Norman Rossington (*Mr Hart*), Gillian Brown (*nun*), Lyn Turner (*streetcrier*)
*Episode 6: 'Golden Apples' only*: Graham Crowden (*Feldkirchner*), Gillian Hills (*Caroline*), John Ringham (*Dr Rasp*), Roger Hammond (*Father Balbi*)
Approximately 55 minutes each episode, colour

## 1972

### Follow the Yellow Brick Road

A BBC Television production for The Sextet series
BBC 2, 4 July

*Producer*: Roderick Graham
*Director*: Alan Bridges
*Designer*: Spencer Chapman
*Script editor*: Margaret Hare
*Film cameraman*: Brian Tufano
*Cast*: Denholm Elliott (*Jack Black*), Billie Whitelaw (*Judy Black*), Richard Vernon (*Dr Whitman*), Dennis Waterman (*Dr Bilson*), Bernard Hepton (*Colin*), Michele Dotrice (*Veronica*), Ruth Dunning (*old lady*), Nicolette Pendrell (*nurse*), Maureen Nelson (*staff nurse*)
70 minutes, colour

## 1973

### Only Make Believe
A BBC Television production for the Play for Today series
BBC 1, 12 February
*Producer*: Graeme McDonald
*Director*: Robert Knights
*Designer*: Graham Oakley
*Script editor*: Ann Scott
*Cast*: Keith Barron (*Christopher Hudson*), Georgina Hale (*Sandra George*), Rowena Cooper (*Cynthia Nicholls*), Alun Armstrong (*Michael Biddle*), Geoffrey Palmer (*Richard Nicholls*), Laurence Hardy (*doctor*), Susan Richards (*Mrs Cawser*), George Howe (*Mr Cawser*), John Malcolm (*interviewer*), Monica Ringwald (*interviewee*)
75 minutes, colour

### A Tragedy of Two Ambitions
A BBC Television production for the Wessex Tales series, based on the story by Thomas Hardy
BBC 2, 21 November
*Producer*: Irene Shubik
*Director*: Michael Tuçhner
*Designer*: Richard Henry
*Film editor*: Ken Pearce
*Film cameraman*: Peter Hall
*Cast*: Paul Rogers (*Mr Harlborough*), John Hurt (*Joshua Harlborough*), David Troughton (*Cornelius Harlborough*), Lynne Frederick (*Rosa Harlborough*), Heather Canning (*Selimar*), Edward Petherbridge (*Squire Fellmer*), Betty Cooper (*Mrs Fellmer*), Dan Meaden (*countryman*), Andrew McCulloch (*farm labourer*), John Rainer (*clergyman*), Peter Bennett (*principal*)
50 minutes, colour

## 1974

### Joe's Ark
A BBC Television production for the Play for Today series
BBC 1, 14 February
*Producer*: Graeme McDonald
*Director*: Alan Bridges

*Designer*: Stuart Walker
*Script editor*: Ann Scott
*Cast*: Freddie Jones (*Joe*), Angharad Rees (*Lucy*), Dennis Waterman (*Bobby*), Christopher Guard (*John*), Patricia Franklin (*Sally*), Edward Evans (*preacher*), Azad Ali (*waiter*), Colin Rix (*chef*), Clive Graham (*doctor*)
65 minutes, colour

## Schmoedipus

A BBC Television production for the Play for Today series
BBC 1, 20 June
*Producer*: Kenith Trodd
*Director*: Barry Davis
*Designer*: Peter Seddon
*Cast*: Anna Cropper (*Elizabeth Carter*), John Carson (*Tom Carter*), Tim Curry (*Glen*), John Horsley (*Ronnie*), Bob Hoskins (*Blake*), Carol Macready (*Dorothy*), Reg Cranfield (*man in corridor*)
67 minutes, colour

## 1975

## Late Call

A BBC Television production, based on the novel by Angus Wilson
BBC 2, 1–22 March
*Producer*: Ken Riddington
*Director*: Philip Dudley
*Designer*: Spencer Chapman
*Script editor*: Lennox Phillips
*Film cameraman*: A. A. Englander
*Film editor*: Sheila Tomlinson
*Cast*: Dandy Nichols (*Sylvia Lennox*), Leslie Dwyer (*Arthur Calvert*), Michael Bryant (*Howard Calvert*), Rosalyn Elvin (*Judy Calvert*), Tim Morand (*Ray Calvert*), Nigel Crewe (*Mark Calvert*), Danielle Carson (*young Sylvia*), Sarah Sutton (*Myra Longmore*), Elizabeth Chambers (*Mrs Longmore*), Mary Chester (*Sylvia's mother*), Geoffrey Adams (*Chris Milton*), Fanny Cosby (*Lorna Milton*), Rosemarie Dunham (*Muriel Bartley*), Nicholas McArdle (*Geoff Bartley*)
*Episode 1 only*: John Dawson (*Mr Martineau*), Patricia Mort (*Pat*), Anne Blake (*Mrs Amherst*), Edward Brooks (*farmer in cart*), Peter Vaughan-Clarke (*farmer's boy*), Jean Anderson (*old woman's voice*), Derek Benfield (*voice of Sylvia's father*), Richard Easton (*doctor's voice*)
*Episode 2 only*: Arthur Lovegrove (*older furniture man*), Frank Jarvis (*younger furniture man*), James Appleby (*Jack Cranston*), Shirley Cain (*Renée Cranston*), Maxine Casson (*Caroline Ogilvie*)
*Episode 3 only*: Alison Griffin (*June*)
*Episode 4 only*: Philip Bond (*Timbo Egan*), Kathryn Leigh Scott (*Shirley Egan*), Hilary Minster (*Dr Piggott*), John Cater (*Herbert Raven*)
Approximately 50 minutes each episode, colour

## 1976

### Double Dare

A BBC Television production for the Play for Today series
BBC 1, 6 April
*Producer*: Kenith Trodd
*Director*: John Mackenzie
*Designer*: Paul Joel
*Film cameraman*: Philip Bonham-Carter
*Film editor*: Roger Waugh
*Cast*: Alan Dobie (*Martin*), Kika Markham (*Helen/Carol*), Malcolm Ferris (*client*), Joe Melia (*Ben*), John Hamill (*Peter*), Elaine Donnelly (*maid*), John Joyce (*barman*), Stanley Lebor (*waiter*), Sarah Nash (*receptionist*), Linda Beckett (*client's wife*), Colin Prockter (*porter*), Ian Munro (*security guard*)
70 minutes, colour

### Brimstone and Treacle

A BBC Television production
BBC 1, produced in 1976, not transmitted until 25 August 1987
*Producer*: Kenith Trodd
*Director*: Barry Davis
*Designer*: Colin Shaw
*Film cameraman*: Peter Bartlett
*Film editor*: Tony Woollard
*Cast*: Denholm Elliott (*Mr Bates*), Michael Kitchen (*Martin*), Patricia Lawrence (*Mrs Bates*), Michelle Newell (*Pattie*), Paul Williamson (*businessman*), Esmond Webb (*man with dog*), Patricia Quayle (*woman in street*), James Greene (*man in street*)
70 minutes, colour

### Where Adam Stood

A BBC Television production, based on *Father and Son* by Edmund Gosse
BBC 2, 21 April
*Producer*: Kenith Trodd
*Director*: Brian Gibson
*Designer*: Gerry Scott
*Cameraman*: Peter Bartlett
*Film editor*: David Martin
*Cast*: Alan Badel (*Philip Gosse*), Max Harris (*Edmund Gosse*), Ronald Hines (*Charles Kingsley*), Heather Canning (*Miss Marks*), Gareth Forwood (*Mr Brackley*), Jean Boht (*Mary Teague*), Hubert Rees (*wagonette driver*)
75 minutes, colour

## 1978

### The Mayor of Casterbridge

A BBC Television production, based on the novel by Thomas Hardy
BBC 2, 22 January–5 March
*Producer*: Jonathan Powell
*Director*: David Giles
*Designer*: Peter Kindred

*Script editor*: Betty Willingale
*Photography*: Hubert Cartwright
*Videotape editor*: Neil Pillaway
*Music*: Carl Davis
*Cast*: Alan Bates (*Michael Henchard*), Anne Stallybrass (*Susan Henchard*), Janet Maw (*Elizabeth Henchard*), Anna Massey (*Lucetta Templeman*), Jack Galloway (*Farfrae*), Avis Bunnage (*Mrs Goodenough*), Richard Owens (*Newson*), Peter Bourke (*Abel Whittle*), Jeffrey Holland (*Carter*), Deddie Davis (*Nancy*), Clifford Parrish (*Longways*), Douglas Milvain (*Concy*), Mischa de la Motte (*priest*), Patricia Fincham (*Henchard's maid*), Ronald Lacey (*Jopp*), Freddie Jones (*Fall*), Gilly Brown (*Lucetta's maid*), Alan Rowe (*Mr Joyce*)
*Episode 1 only*: Anthony Douse (*turnip hoer*), Rod Beacham (*man at fair*), Bernard Taylor (*second man at fair*), Leonard Trolley (*auctioneer*), Terry Francis (*waiter*), Denis Costello (*guest*)
*Episode 2 only*: Joe Ritchie (*Buzzford*), Stuart Fell (*man at fête*), Steven Warner (*boy*), Anthony Spicer (*farmer*), Arthur Bridgeman (*second farmer*)
*Episode 4 only*: Kenneth Waller (*clerk of court*), David Anker (*policeman*)
*Episode 5 only*: William Whymper (*commissioner*), Michael Miller (*farmer*), John Flint (*landlord*), Jack Le White (*fiddler*), Phillada Sewell (*old woman*)
*Episode 6 only*: Desmond Adams (*Charl*), Lloyd McGuire (*Prince Albert*), Charles West (*doctor*), David Willitts (*councillor*)
*Episode 7 only*: Alan Collins (*labourer*), Alec Bregonzi (*companion*), Trudie Styler (*cook*)
Approximately 55 minutes each episode, colour

## Pennies from Heaven

Subtitled 'Six Plays With Music'
A BBC Television production
BBC 1, 7 March–11 April
*Producer*: Kenith Trodd
*Director*: Piers Haggard
*Designers*: Tim Harvey, Bruce Macadie
*Film editor*: David Martin
*Film photography*: Ken Westbury
*Songs*: 'Seein' is Believing' by Adams, Ager, 'Pop! Goes Your Heart' by Dixon, Wrubel, 'Haunting Me' by de Lange, Myrow (vocals all three Alan Kane), 'Zing! Went the Strings of my Heart' by Hanley (vocals Joe Crossman, Alfie Noakes, Don Barrigo, Jack Jacobsen), 'Anything Goes' by Porter (vocals the Radio Three), 'Pick Yourself Up' by Kern, Fields (vocals Bert Yarlett), 'Cheek to Cheek' by Berlin (vocals Sam Browne), 'I Love You Truly' by Jacobs, Bond, 'Easy Come, Easy Go' by Green, Heyman, 'Hand in Hand' by Kern, Hammerstein, 'You Couldn't Be Cuter' and 'Just Let Me Look at You' by Kern, Fields, 'Isn't it Heavenly' by Harburg, Meyer, 'My Woman' by Crosby, Wallman, Wartel, 'Riptide' by Kahn, Donaldson (vocals all eight Al Bowlly), 'That's a-Plenty' by Pollack, Gilbert, 'Maybe I'm Wrong Again' by Brent, Bennett, 'The Glory of Love' by Hill, 'Garden of Weed' by Foresythe, 'Oh Susannah' by Foster, performed by Lew Stone and his Orchestra; 'Love is the Sweetest Thing' by Noble, 'Roll Along Prairie Moon' by Fiorito, Mac-Pherson, Von Tilzer, 'Fancy our Meeting' by Meyer, Charig, Furber, performed by Al Bowlly and Orchestra; 'You Rascal, You' by Theard, performed by Joe Crossman and the Blue Lyres; 'Down Sunnyside Lane' by Campbell, Connelly, performed by Jack Payne and his BBC Dance Orchestra; 'Yes Yes (My Baby Said "Yes")' by Conrad, Friend (vocals Sam

Browne and the Carlyle Cousins), 'Whistling in the Dark' by Suesse (vocals Sam Browne), 'The Clouds Will Soon Roll By' by Woods, Dixon, 'You've Got Me Crying Again' by Newman, Jones (vocals on both Elsie Carlisle), 'Painting the Clouds with Sunshine' by Dubin, Burke (vocals Male Trio), performed by Ambrose and his Orchestra; 'I Like to Go Back in the Evening' by Pascoe, Clint, Williams, O'Reilly (vocals Fred Latham), 'Roll Along Prairie Moon', 'I Found the Right Girl' by Lupino, Gay, performed by Jack Jackson and his Orchestra; 'Blue Moon' by Rodgers, Hart, performed by Greta Keller and the Victor Young Orchestra; 'Smoke Gets in your Eyes' by Harbach, Kern, performed by Phyllis Robins and Orchestra; 'Pennies from Heaven' and 'So Do I' by Burke, Johnston, performed by the Street Singer (Arthur Tracy); 'You and the Night and the Music' by Dietz, Schwartz, performed by Dan Donovan and Debroy Somers Band; 'Love is Good for Anything that Ails You' by Malneck, Friend (vocals Evelyn Dall), performed by Orlando and his Orchestra; 'Dreaming a Dream' by Waller, Tunbridge, Weston-Lee (vocals Al Bowlly), 'Oh You Nasty Man' by Yellen, Caesar, Henderson (vocals Dorothy Carless), performed by Ray Noble and his Orchestra; 'Radio Times' by Hall, 'How's Chances' by Berlin, 'Hands across the Table' by Parish, Delettre, performed by Dan Donovan and the BBC Dance Orchestra, directed by Henry Hall; 'Life Begins at Oxford Circus' by Nicholls, 'Painting the Clouds with Sunshine' performed by Jack Hylton and his Orchestra; 'I Only Have Eyes for You' by Dubin, Warren, performed by Jack Plant and Scott Wood and his Orchestra; 'We'll Make Hay while the Sun Shines' by Freed, Brown, performed by Billy Merrin and his Commanders; 'Better Think Twice' by Seymour, Coots, 'The Moon Got in My Eyes' by Burke, Johnston (vocals Anne Lenner), performed by Carroll Gibbons and the Savoy Hotel Orpheans; 'Indian Love Call' by Harbach, Hammerstein, Friml (vocals Sam Costa, Judy Shirley), performed by Maurice Winnick and his Orchestra; 'Okay Toots' by Kahn, Donaldson, 'Roll Along Prairie Moon' (vocals Ivor Moreton), 'Roll Along Covered Wagon' by Kennedy (vocals Bill Currie), performed by Harry Roy and his Orchestra; 'It's Got to be Love' by Rodgers, Hart (vocals Mary Lee), 'The Echo of a Song' by Mendoza (vocals Al Bowlly), 'On the Other Side of the Hill' by Kennedy, 'In the Dark' by Hill, Bergman, 'Roll Along Prairie Moon' (vocals all three Denny Dennis), 'Without That Certain Thing' by Nesbit, Nesbit (vocals Peggy Dell), performed by Roy Fox and his Orchestra; 'Serenade in the Night' by Bixio, Cheryubin, Kennedy (vocals Ronnie Hill), medley: 'Roll Along Prairie Moon', 'Pennies from Heaven', performed by Primo Scala's Accordion Band; 'You Sweet So and So' by Furber, Gershwin, Meyer, Charig, performed by Jack Buchanan; 'On the Sunny Side of the Street,' performed by George Earbrass; 'Says My Heart' by Loesser, Lane (vocals Eve Becke), 'Pennies from Heaven' (vocals Edward Molloy), performed by Louis Levy and his Gaumont British Orchestra; 'Says My Heart', performed by Brian Lawrence Orchestra; 'In the Middle of a Kiss' by Coslow, performed by Connie Boswell and Orchestra, also by Charlie Kunz and Orchestra; 'March Winds and April Showers' by Samuels, Whitcup, Powell (vocals Eric Whitley), performed by Teddy Joyce and his Orchestra; 'Pennies from Heaven', performed by Turner Layton; 'There is a Green Hill Far Away', 'Rock of Ages', 'The Old Rugged Cross', 'Pennies from Heaven' played on accordion by Henry Krein; medley: 'Moon' by Caleo, Miles, 'Blue Moon', 'Shine on Harvest Moon' by Boyes, Norworth, 'Me and the Moon' by Monaco, 'What a Little Moonlight Can Do' by Woods, 'If the Moon Turns Green' by Hanighen, 'Moon Country' by Carmichael, Mercer, 'The Moon was Yellow' by Anhert, played by Sam Avent (piano); medley: 'I'm in the Mood for Love' by McHugh, Fields, 'The Very Thought of You' by Noble, 'Tip-toe Through the Tulips' by Burke, 'Painting the Clouds with Sunshine', performed by Brian Dee (piano), Neville Hughes (violin); 'All Things Bright and Beautiful', sung by children from the Forest of Dean

*Cast*: Bob Hoskins (*Arthur Parker*), Gemma Craven (*Joan Parker*), Kenneth Colley (*the accordion man*), Cheryl Campbell (*Eileen Everson*), Arnold Peters (*Barrett*), Sam Avent (*pianist*), Jenny Logan (*Irene*), Freddie Jones (*headmaster*), Spencer Banks (*Maurice*), Michael Bilten (*Dad*), Philip Jackson (*Dave*), Bill Dean (*Alf*), Bella Emberg (*Mrs Corder*), Dave King (*police inspector*)
*Episode 1: 'Down Sunnyside Lane' only*: Nigel Havers (*Conrad Baker*), Rosemary Martin (*Marjorie*), Robert Putt (*Jumbo*), Keith Marsh (*Will*), Tessa Dunne (*Betty*), Wally Thomas (*Carter*)
*Episode 2: 'The Sweetest Thing' only*: Peter Cellier (*bank manager*), Cyril Cross (*customer*), Roger Sloman (*Ted*)
*Episode 3: 'Easy Come, Easy Go' only*: Frederick Bradley (*miner*), Maryann Turner (*woman patient*), Yolande Palfrey (*blind girl*), Roger Forbes (*police constable*), John Malcolm (*detective inspector*)
*Episode 4: 'Better Think Twice' only*: Tony Caunter (*café proprietor*), Tudor Davies (*café customer*), Hywel Bennett (*Tom*)
*Episode 5: 'Painting the Clouds' only*: Paddy Joyce (*tramp*), Nigel Rathbone (*Michael*), Ronald Fraser (*Major Archibald Paxville*), Reg Lever (*man in queue*), Ronnie Ross (*busker*), Alan Foss (*waiter*), Chris Gannon (*man on bridge*), Laurence Harrington (*second inspector*), David Webb (*shop manager*), Robin Meredith (*customer*)
*Episode 6: 'Says my Heart' only*: Steve Ubels (*pedestrian*), Philip Locke (*farmer*), John Ringham (*sergeant*), Tim Swinton (*constable*), Carleton Hobbs (*judge*), Peter Bowles (*prosecuting counsel*), Stanley Fleet (*clerk of the court*)
Approximately 70 minutes each episode, colour

## 1979

### Blue Remembered Hills
A BBC Television production for the Play for Today series
BBC 1, 30 January
*Producer*: Kenith Trodd
*Director*: Brian Gibson
*Designer*: Richard Henry
*Photography*: Nat Crosby
*Cast*: Colin Welland (*Willie*), Michael Elphick (*Peter*), Robin Ellis (*John*), John Bird (*Raymond*), Helen Mirren (*Angela*), Janine Duvitski (*Audrey*), Colin Jeavons (*'Donald Duck'*), Dennis Potter (*narrator of verse, voice only*)
72 minutes, colour

## 1980

### Blade on the Feather
An LWT production in association with Pennies From Heaven Ltd
ITV, 19 October
*Executive producer*: Tony Wharmby
*Producer*: Kenith Trodd
*Assistant producer*: Jerry Desmonde
*Director*: Richard Loncraine
*Designer*: Andrew Drummond
*Assistant designer*: James Dillon

Photography: Peter Hannan
Film editor: Jon Costelloe
Cast: Donald Pleasence (Jason Cavendish), Tom Conti (Daniel Young), Denholm Elliott (Hill), Kika Markham (Linda Cavendish), Phoebe Nicholls (Christabel Cavendish), Gareth Forwood (doctor), Bill Weston (Andrew Cartwright), Joel Samuel (young Daniel), Alvar Lidell (newsreader)
78 minutes, colour

## Rain on the Roof
An LWT production in association with Pennies From Heaven Ltd
ITV, 26 October
Executive producer: Tony Wharmby
Producer: Kenith Trodd
Assistant producer: Jerry Desmonde
Director: Alan Bridges
Designer: Bryan Bagge
Photography: Michael Reed
Film editor: Ray Helm
Cast: Cheryl Campbell (Janet), Malcolm Stoddard (John), Michael Culver (Malcolm), Madelinde Hinde (Emma), Ewan Stewart (Billy), William Bond (Billy's father), Alan Cullen (vicar), Dave Royal (postman), David Webb (Mr Castle)
78 minutes, colour

## Cream in my Coffee
An LWT production in association with Pennies From Heaven Ltd
ITV, 2 November
Executive producer: Tony Wharmby
Producer: Kenith Trodd
Director: Gavin Millar
Designer: John Emery
Photography: Ernest Vincze
Film editor: Derek Bain
Cast: Lionel Jeffries (Bernard Wilsher), Peggy Ashcroft (Jean Wilsher), Peter Chelsom (young Bernard), Shelagh McLeod (young Jean), Martin Shaw (Jack Butcher), Faith Brook (Mrs Wilsher), Leo Dollan (hotel porter, present), Will Stampe (hotel porter, past), Tracy Eddon (girl in pool), Dawn Perllman (waitress, past), Walter Sparrow (boatman), Howard Attfield (waiter), Robert Fyfe (vicar), Famous Names (rock group)
78 minutes, colour

## 1985
### Tender is the Night
A BBC Television production in association with Showtime Entertainment and The Seven Network, Australia, by arrangement with 20th Century-Fox, based on the novel by F. Scott Fitzgerald
BBC 2, 23 September–28 October
Executive producer: Jonathan Powell
Producer: Betty Willingale
Director: Robert Knights

*Designers*: Derek Dodd, Peter Higgins
*Photography*: Ken Westbury
*Film editor*: Tariq Anwar
*Original music*: Richard Rodney Bennett
*Cast*: Peter Strauss (*Dick Diver*), Mary Steenburgen (*Nicole Warren*), Sean Young (*Rosemary Hoyt*), John Heard (*Abe North*), Joris Stuyck (*Tommy Barban*), Edward Asner (*Devereux Warren*), Jurgen Brugger (*Franz Gregorovius*), Astrid Frank (*Kaethe Gregorovius*), Kate Harper (*Baby Warren*), Nancy Paul (*Mary North*), Dennis Creaghan (*Albert McKisco*), Toria Fuller (*Violet McKisco*), Terrance Conder (*Royal Dumphry*), Joanna David (*Hannah*)
*Episode 1 only*: Erwin Kohlund (*Dr Dohmler*), Richard Linford (*wounded soldier*), Jean Alonge (*singing soldier*), Keith Edwards (*major in train*), Rosario Serrano (*Spanish woman patient*), François Guetary (*Conte di Marmora*)
*Episode 2 only*: Piper Laurie (*Mrs Speers*), Vernon Dobtcheef (*Luis Campion*), Mary Ellen Ray (*Mrs Abrams*), Pierre Castello (*French second*), André Chaumeau (*French doctor*)
*Episode 3 only*: Linsey Beauchamp (*girl at cemetery*), Tacy Kneale (*Maria Wallis*), Stephane Freiss (*Sergeant de Ville*), Ruddy L. David (*Jules Peterson*)
*Episode 4 only*: Erin Donovan (*Helen*), Barbara Atkinson (*English woman patient*), Pat Starr (*Helen's mother*), Norman Stokle (*preacher at graveside*)
*Episode 5 only*: Hutton Cobb (*Collis Clay*), Marc-Samuel Hadjadj (*Nicotera*), Frank Karla (*film director*), Matt Frewer, Rolf Saxon, William Hope (*Americans in bar*), Teco Celio (*Rome taxi driver*), David Pontremoli (*Rome police officer*)
*Episode 6 only*: Jerome Willis (*T. E. Golding*), Amanda Hillwood (*Lady Caroline Sibley-Biers*), John Sessions (*young Scot*)
Approximately 55 minutes each episode, colour

## 1986

### The Singing Detective

A BBC Television production in association with Australian Broadcasting Corporation
BBC 1, 16 November–21 December
*Producers*: Kenith Trodd, John Harris
*Director*: Jon Amiel
*Designer*: Jim Clay
*Photography*: Ken Westbury
*Film editors*: Sue Wyatt (episodes 1, 3, 5), Bill Wright (episodes 2, 4, 6)
*Music*: Max Harris
*Cast*: Michael Gambon (*Philip E. Marlow*), Janet Suzman (*Nicola*), Patrick Malahide (*Mark Binney/Finney/Raymond*), Joanne Whalley (*Nurse Mills*), Bill Paterson (*Dr Gibbon*), Jim Carter (*Mr Marlow*), Alison Steadman (*Mrs Marlow/Lili*), Lyndon Davies (*young Philip*), David Ryall (*Mr Hall*), Gerard Horan (*Reginald*), Imelda Staunton (*Staff Nurse White*), Mary McLeod (*Sister Malone*), Ron Cook (*first mysterious man*), George Rossi (*second mysterious man*), Geff Francis (*hospital porter*), Sharon D. Clarke (*night nurse*), Kate McKenzie (*Sonia*), Charon Bourke (*Amanda*), Simon Chandler (*Dr Finlay*), Leslie French (*Mr Tomkey, 'Noddy'*), Charles Simon (*George Adams*), Janet Henfrey (*schoolteacher/scarecrow*)
*Episode 1: 'Skin' only*: Badi Uzzaman (*Ali*), Nigel Pegram (*busker*), Richard Pescud (*consultant*), Thomas Wheatley (*registrar*), Paul Lacoux (*houseman*), John Matshikiza (*visiting doctor*)

*Songs*: 'Peg o' my Heart' (series title music) by Fisher, Bryan, performed by Max Harris and his Novelty Trio; 'Limehouse Blues' by Furber, Braham, performed by Ambrose and his Orchestra; 'Deutschland über Alles' by Hoffman, Fullersleben, soloist Tommy Riley; 'House of Mystery'; 'I've Got You under my Skin' by Porter, performed by Henry Hall Orchestra; 'Blues in the Night' by Arlen, Mercer, performed by Anne Shelton; 'Sunnyside of the Street' by Fields, McHugh; 'Entry of the Queen of Sheba' by G. F. Handel, performed by Christopher Hogwood; 'Dry Bones' by Livingstone Gearhart, performed by Fred Waring and the Pennsylvanians; 'Night and Day' by Porter; 'Rockin' in Rhythm' by Ellington, Carney, Mills, performed by Duke Ellington and his Famous Orchestra.

*Episode 2*: 'Heat' only: Joan White (*Mrs Adams*), Richard Butler (*Grancher*), Maggie Holland (*Gran*)

*Songs*: 'Cruising Down the River' by Beadell, Tolleaton, performed by Michael Gambon, also by Lou Preager and his Orchestra, with Paul Rich: 'Don't Fence Me In' by Porter, performed by Bing Crosby and the Andrews Sisters; 'It Might as Well be Spring' by Rodgers, Hammerstein, performed by Dick Haymes; 'Rustle of Spring' by Sinding, performed by Joseph Cooper; 'Rockin' in Rhythm'; 'Birdsong at Eventide' by Coates, performed by Ronnie Ronalde

*Episode 3*: 'Lovely Days' only: Errol Shaker (*first mortuary attendant*), Astley Harvey (*second mortuary attendant*), Claire Phelps (*Rita*), Neil Pittaway (*Brian*)

*Songs*: 'Paper Doll' by Black, performed by Mills Brothers; 'Lili Marlene' by Schultze, Leip, Connor, performed by Lale Anderson; 'Do I Worry' by Cowan, Worth, performed by the Ink Spots

*Episode 4*: 'Clues' only: Ken Stott (*Uncle John*), Angela Curran (*Mary*), Heather Tobias (*girl evangelist/Nurse Godfrey*), John Sheraton (*drummer*), Emma Myant (*first hostess*), Susie Ann Watkins (*second hostess*)

*Songs*: 'Lili Marlene' performed by Lale Anderson; 'Bei mir bist du schön' by Secunda, Cahn, Chaplin, Jacobs, performed by Maurice Winnick and his Sweet Music; 'Rockin' in Rhythm'; 'It's a Lovely Day Tomorrow' by Berlin, performed by Jack Payne and his Orchestra; 'I Get Along without You Very Well' by Carmichael, performed by Sam Browne with Lew Stone Band; 'Life at Best is Very Brief' by Kirkpatrick, organist Dennis Plowright; 'Ac-cent-tchu-ate the Positive' by Arlen, Mercer, performed by Bing Crosby and the Andrews Sisters

*Episode 5*: 'Pitter Patter'

*Songs*: 'The Umbrella Man' by Rose, Stock, Cavanagh, performed by Sammy Kaye and his Orchestra with the Three Barons; 'Henrietta' by Featherstonchaugh, performed by Buddy Featherstonehaugh; 'You Always Hurt the One You Love' by Roberts, Fisher, performed by Mills Brothers; 'Ah! Sweet Mystery of Life' by Herbert, Young, performed by Ambrose and his Orchestra

*Episode 6*: 'Who Done It' only: Tricia George (*physiotherapist*), Samantha Bryant (*Barbara*)

*Songs*: 'After You've Gone' by Creamer, Layton, performed by Al Jolson; 'Into Each Life Some Rain Must Fall' by Roberts, Fisher, performed by Ella Fitzgerald and the Ink Spots; 'Putting on the Ritz' by Berlin, performed by Eric Rogers; 'The Very Thought of You' by Noble, performed by Al Bowlly with the Ray Noble Orchestra; 'The Teddy Bears' Picnic' by Kennedy, Bratton, performed by Henry Hall and his Orchestra; 'Peg o' my Heart', soloist Tommy Reilly; 'We'll Meet Again' by Parker, Charles, performed by Vera Lynn with Arthur Young at the Novachord

Approximately 70 minutes each episode, colour

## 1987

### Visitors

A BBC Television production in association with Polymuse and W. W. Entertainment for the Screen Two series
BBC 2, 22 February
*Producer*: Kenith Trodd
*Director*: Piers Haggard
*Photography*: John Else
*Designer*: Derek Dodd
*Script editor*: Sarah Curtis
*Film editor*: Ken Pearce
*Cast*: Michael Brandon (*Eddie*), Glynis Barber (*Lucy*), John Standing (*Jack*), Nicola Pagett (*Elizabeth*), Robert MacNaughton (*Clayton*), Mary Minniti (*maid*), Christiana Sartoretti, Enrico Masciolini, Giorgio Pangaro (*watchers*)
90 minutes, colour

## 1988

### Christabel

Subtitled 'A Film in Four Parts by Dennis Potter'
A BBC Television production in association with Arts & Entertainment Network, based on *The Past is Myself* by Christabel Bielenberg
BBC 2, 16 November–7 December
*Executive Producer*: Dennis Potter
*Producer*: Kenith Trodd
*Director*: Adrian Shergold
*Photography*: Remi Adefarasin
*Designer*: Jim Clay
*Film editor*: Clare Douglas
*Original music*: Stanley Myers
*Cast*: Elizabeth Hurley (*Christabel Burton/Bielenberg*), Stephen Dillon (*Peter Bielenberg*), Geoffrey Palmer (*Mr Burton*), Ann Bell (*Mrs Burton*), Nigel Le Vaillant (*Adam Von Trott*), Suzan Crowley (*Lexi*), Jim Carter (*Bausch*), Pat Heywood (*Frau Muckle*), Sam Kelly (*Langbehn*), David Lyon (*Kreuze*), John Burgess (*Neisse*), Renny Lister (*Aunt Ulla*), Nicola Wright (*Clarita Von Trott*), John Boswall (*Alois*)
*Episode 1 only*: Robert Howard (*priest*), Guy Deghy (*Professor Bauer*), John Barrard (*Jewish tailor*)
*Episode 2 only*: Jessica Turner (*Ilse*), Adrian Rawlins (*Albrecht*), Greg Crutwell (*young soldier in park*)
*Episode 3 only*: Richard Ireson (*Volk*), Dennis Christopher (*US airman*), Andrew Wilde (*SS man*), Joanne Allen (*Frau Lange*)
*Episode 4 only*: Ralph Brown (*Lange*), Edna Dore (*old lady*)
Approximately 55 minutes each episode, colour

## 1989

### Blackeyes

A BBC Television production in association with Australian Broadcasting Corporation and Television New Zealand, based on the novel by Dennis Potter

BBC 2, 19 November–20 December
*Producer*: Rick McCallum
*Associate producer*: Kathryn Farrar
*Director*: Dennis Potter
*Designer*: Geoff Powell
*Photography*: Andrew Dunn
*Film editor*: Clare Douglas with Michael Parker
*Music*: Max Harris
*Cast*: Michael Gough (*Maurice James Kingsley*), Carol Royle (*Jessica*), Nigel Planer (*Jeff*), Gina Bellman (*Blackeyes*), John Shrapnel (*Detective Blake*), Colin Jeavons (*Jamieson*), Nicholas Woodeson (*Stilk*), Hannah Morris (*little Jessica*), David Westhead (*Mark Wilsher*), Dennis Potter (*narrator, voice only*)
*Episode 1 only*: Cyril Shaps (*pathologist*), Ann Bell (*casting director*), Lee Simpson (*constable*)
*Episode 2 only*: Dennis Lotis (*singer*)
*Episode 3 only*: Gary Love (*Colin*), Charles Gray (*Sebastian*), Ian Gelder (*Rupert*), Peter Birch (*Charles*), Samantha Gates (*receptionist*), Christopher Guard (*John Bennon*), Nikki Mace (*model*), Lucinda Fisher (*Bennon's assistant*)
*Episode 4 only*: Laurence Rudic (*commercial director*), Roger Walker (*Bert*), Tracey Eddon, Eddie Eddon (*stunt co-ordinators*)
Approximately 50 minutes each episode, colour

## 1993

### Lipstick on your Collar

A Whistling Gypsy Production for Channel 4 Television
Channel 4, 21 February–28 March
*Executive producer*: Dennis Potter
*Producer*: Rosemarie Whitman
*Co-producer*: Alison Barnett
*Director*: Renny Rye
*Designer*: Gary Williamson
*Photography*: Sean Van Hales
*Film editor*: Clare Douglas
*Cast*: Giles Thomas (*Private Francis Francis*), Louise Germaine (*Sylvia Berry*), Ewan McGregor (*Private Mick Hopper*), Kymberley Huffman (*Lisa*), Nicholas Farrell (*Major Johnny Church*), Peter Jeffrey (*Lt-Col. Harry Bernwood*), Nicholas Jones (*Major Archie Carter*), Shane Rimmer (*Lt-Col. 'Truck' Trekker*), Douglas Henshall (*Lance Corporal Peter Berry*), Clive Francis (*Major Wallace Hedges*), Carrie Leigh (*Angel/Eve*), Maggie Steed (*Aunt Vickie*), Roy Hudd (*Harold Atterbow*), Bernard Hill (*Uncle Fred*)
*Episode 1 only*: Damian Dibben (*young man in cinema*)
*Songs*: 'Lipstick on your Collar' performed by Connie Francis; 'The Great Pretender' performed by The Platters; 'Earth Angel' performed by the Crewcuts; 'Little Bitty Pretty One' performed by Thirston Harris; 'The Garden of Eden' performed by Frankie Vaughan with Wally Stott, his Orchestra and Chorus; 'The Green Door' performed by Frankie Vaughan with the Wally Stott Orchestra
*Episode 2 only*: Frederick Treves (*Brigadier Sanders*)
*Songs*: 'Only You (And You Alone)' and 'My Prayer' performed by the Platters; 'The Story of my Life' performed by Michael Holliday; 'Blueberry Hill' performed by Fats Domino;

'It's Almost Tomorrow' performed by the Dreamweavers; 'Don't be Cruel' performed by Elvis Presley; 'Your Cheatin' Heart' performed by Hank Williams; organ music: 'In a Persian Market Place'; 'Destiny Waltz'

*Episode 3 only*: John Cater (*Mr Shepherd, bookshop owner*), Debra Beaumont ('*Nina*'), James Snell ('*Trigorin*'), Bernard Brown (*voice of Anthony Eden*)

*Songs*: 'Blue Suede Shoes' performed by Carl Perkins; 'Raining in my Heart' performed by Buddy Holly and the Crickets; organ music: 'In a Monstery Garden'; 'The Whistler and his Dog'

*Episode 4 only*: Jay Villiers (*captain*), Jean Fergusson (*Palais dance instructor*), Sean Baker (*Palais manager*), Michael Nielsen (*man at Palais*), Andy Laycock (*1st soldier*), Daniel Ryan (*2nd soldier*)

*Songs*: 'Unchained Melody' performed by Lex Baxter; 'I See the Moon' performed by the Stargazers; 'Be-Bop-a-Lula' performed by Gene Vincent

*Episode 5 only*: Carol Starks ('*Masha*'), Geoffrey Larder ('*Medvedenko*'), Allison Hancock ('*Arkadina*'), Steven Tremblay ('*Sanford Clark*'), Terence Bayler (*general*), Tim Seely (*brigadier*), Jim Carter (*detective inspector*), Benedict Martin (*policeman*)

*Songs*: 'I'm in Love Again' performed by Fats Domino; 'The Fool' performed by Sanford Clark; 'Band of Gold' performed by Don Cherry 'Young Love' performed by Tab Hunter

*Episode 6 only*: Roger Hume (*lt-col.*), Rupert Baker (*senior parachute officer*), Geoffrey Drew (*vicar*), Ysanne Churchman (*Mrs Atterbow*), Che Walker (*policeman*), Wensley Pithey (*elderly gent in club*), Darren Lawrence (*Private Mason*)

*Songs*: 'Robin Hood', performed by Gary Miller with Tony Osborne and his Orchestra and the Beryl Stott Chorus; 'It'll be Me' performed by Jerry Lee Lewis; 'Love is Strange' performed by Mickey and Sylvia; 'Sh 'Boom: Life Could be a Dream' performed by the Crew Cuts; 'Lotta Lovin'' performed by Gene Vincent and the Blue Caps; 'Lay Down your Arms' performed by Anne Shelton

Approximately 58 minutes each episode, colour

## FEATURE FILMS

### 1981

*Pennies from Heaven*

USA; A Hera Production for MGM, based on the television serial by Dennis Potter

*Executive Producer*: Rick McCallum

*Producers*: Nora Kaye, Herbert Ross

*Director*: Herbert Ross

*Associate producer*: Ken Adam

*Set design*: Christopher Burian-Mohr

*Cinematography*: Gordon Willis

*Sound*: Richard L. Anderson, Stephen H. Flick

*Editor*: Richard Marks

*Choreography*: Danny Daniels

*Music director/arranger*: Marvin Hamlisch

*Songs*: 'The Clouds Will Soon Roll By' by Woods, Dixon, performed by Elsie Carlisle with Ambrose and his Orchestra; 'I'll Never Have to Dream Again' by Jones, Newman, performed by Connie Boswell; 'Yes Yes! (My Baby Said "Yes")' by Conrad, Friend, performed by Sam Browne and The Carlyle Cousins; 'Did You Ever See a Dream Walking?' by Revel, Gordon, performed by Bing Crosby; 'Pennies from Heaven' by Burke, Johnston, performed by Arthur Tracy; 'It's the Girl' by Baer, Oppenheim, performed by the Boswell Sisters with the Dorsey Brothers Orchestra; 'Love is Good for Anything that Ails You' by Malneck, Friend, performed by Phyllis Robbins with Orlando and his Orchestra; 'Let's Put Out the Lights and Go to Sleep' by Hupfeld, performed by Rudy Vallee and his Connecticut Yankees; 'It's a Sin to Tell a Lie' by Mayhew, performed by Dolly Dawn with George Hall and his Orchestra; 'I Want to be Bad' by De Sylva, Brown, Henderson, performed by Helen Kane; 'Let's Misbehave' by Porter, performed by Irving Aaronson and his Commanders; 'Life is Just a Bowl of Cherries' by Henderson, Brown, performed by Walt Harrah, Gene Merlino, Vern Rowe, Robert Tebow, Al Vescovo; 'Let's Face the Music and Dance' by Berlin, performed by Fred Astaire

*Film Extract*: *Follow the Fleet* (1936)
*Cast*: Steve Martin (*Arthur Parker*), Bernadette Peters (*Eileen Everson*), Christopher Walken (*Tom*), Jessica Harper (*Joan Parker*), Vernel Bagneris (*the accordion man*), John McMartin (*Mr Warner*), John Karlen (*detective*), Jay Garner (*banker*), Robert Fitch (*Al*), Tommy Rall (*Ed*), Eliska Krupka (*blind girl*), Frank McCarthy (*bartender*), Raleigh Bond (*Mr Barrett*), Gloria Leroy (*prostitute*), Nancy Parsons (*old whore*), Toni Kaye, Shirley Kirkes (*tarts*), Jack Fletcher (*elevator operator*), Hunter Watkins (*boy*), Arell Blanton, George Wilbur (*motorcycle police*), M. C. Gainey (*young policeman*), Mark Campbell (*newsboy*), James Mendenhall (*warden*), Jim Boeke (*hangman*), Will Hare (*Father Everson*), Joshua Cadman (*Jumbo*)
108 minutes, colour

## 1982

### Brimstone and Treacle

UK; Namara Films/Alan E. Salke in association with Herbert Solow. A Pennies From Heaven Film, based on the television play by Dennis Potter
*Executive producer*: Naim Attallah
*Producer*: Kenith Trodd
*Director*: Richard Loncraine
*Production design*: Milly Burns
*Cinematography*: Peter Hannan
*Sound*: Alan Bell
*Editor*: Paul Green
*Music*: Sting, performed by the Police; Michael Nyman
*Songs*: 'We Got the Beat' by Caffey, performed by the Go-Go's; 'Up the Junction' by Difford, Tillbrook, performed by Squeeze; 'Spread a Little Happiness' by Ellis, Grey, Norman, performed by Sting
*Cast*: Sting (*Martin Taylor*), Denholm Elliott (*Thomas Bates*), Joan Plowright (*Norma Bates*), Suzanna Hamilton (*Patricia Bates*), Benjamin Whitrow (*businessman*), Dudley Sutton (*stroller*), Mary McLeod (*Miss Holdsworth*), Tim Preece (*clergyman*), Elizabeth Bradley (*passer-by*), Hugh Walters (*man*), Christopher Fairbanks (*drunk*)
87 minutes, colour

## 1983

### Gorky Park

USA; Eagle Associates for Orion, based on the novel by Martin Cruz Smith
*Executive Producer*: Bob Larson

*Producers*: Gene Kirkwood, Howard W. Koch Jr
*Associate producers*: Efrem Harkham, Uri Harkham
*Director*: Michael Apted
*Production design*: Paul Sylbert
*Cinematography*: Ralf D. Bode
*Sound*: Michael Hilkene
*Editor*: Dennis Virkler
*Music*: '1812 Overture', 'Swan Lake' by Tchaikovsky, orchestrated by Greig McRitchie
*Songs*: 'It's So Easy', by Holly, Petty; 'Twist and Shout' by Russell, Medley
*Cast*: William Hurt (*Arkady Renko*), Lee Marvin (*Jack Osborne*), Brian Dennehy (*William Kirwill*), Ian Bannen (*Iamskov*), Joanna Pacula (*Irina Asanova*), Michael Elphick (*Pasha Pavlovich*), Richard Griffiths (*Anton*), Rikki Fulton (*Major Pribluda*), Alexander Knox (*general*), Alexei Sayle (*Golodkin*), Iain McDiarmid (*Professor Andreev*), Niall O'Brien (*KGB Agent Rurik*), Henry Woolf (*Levin*), Tusse Silberg (*Natasha*), Patrick Field (*Fet*), Jukka Hirvik Angas (*James Kirwill*), Marjatta Nissinen (*Valerva Davidova*), Hekki Leppanen (*Kostia Borodin*), Lauri Torhonen (*director*), Elsa Salamaa (*Babuska*), Anatoly Davydov (*KGB Agent Nicky*), Lasse Lindberg, Jussi Parvianen (*shadowers*), Black Pearls (*Russian tea band*), Bad Sign (*rock band*)
128 minutes, colour

## 1985

### Dreamchild
UK; A PFH FIlm for Thorn EMI Screen Entertainment
*Executive producers*: Dennis Potter, Verity Lambert
*Producers*: Rick McCallum, Kenith Trodd
*Director*: Gavin Millar
*Production designer*: Roger Hall
*Cinematography*: Billy Williams
*Sound*: Godfrey Kirby
*Editor*: Angus Newton
*Music*: Stanley Myers
*Songs/tunes*: 'Speakeasy Blues', 'Tumbleweed Luke Theme', 'Smoke Signal', 'Suspense Links', 'Will You Won't You', 'Columbia Fanfare', 'Rule, Britannia', 'Ash Grove'
*Animatronics*: Jim Henson's Creature Shop
*Cast*: Coral Browne (*Mrs Hargreaves*), Ian Holm (*Revd Charles Dodgson*), Peter Gallagher (*Jack Dolan*), Chris Corfman (*Sally Mackeson*), Nicola Cowper (*Lucy*), Jane Asher (*Mrs Liddell*), Amelia Shankley (*little Alice*), Imogen Boorman (*Lorina*), Emma King (*Edith*), Rupert Wainwright (*Hargreaves*), Roger Ashton-Griffiths (*Revd Duckworth*), James Wilby (*Baker*), Shane Rimmer (*Mr Marl*), Peter Whitman (*radio producer*), Ken Campbell (*radio sound effects man/voice of March Hare*), William Hootkins (*1st radio actor*), Jeffrey Chiswick (*2nd radio actor*), Pat Starr (*radio actress*), Johnny M. (*1st crooner*), Alan Sherman (*1st reporter*), Danny Brannin (*3rd reporter/photographer*), Sam Douglas (*4th reporter*), Peter Banks (*1st editor*), Derek Hoxby (*2nd editor*), Ron Berglas (*3rd editor*), Ron Travis (*4th editor*), Thomasine Heiner (*announcer/chairman*), Olivier Pierre (*president of university*), Tony Mansell (*Waldorf Astoria crooner*). Voices only: Fulton Mackay (*Gryphon*), Alan Bennett (*Mock Turtle*), Julie Walters (*Dormouse*), Tony Haygarth (*Mad Hatter*), Frank Middlemass (*Caterpillar*)

90 minutes, colour

## 1987
### Track 29
UK; HandMade Films
*Executive producers*: George Harrison, Denis O'Brien
*Producer*: Rick McCallum
*Director*: Nicolas Roeg
*Production designer*: David Brockhurst
*Cinematography*: Alex Thomson
*Sound*: Rodney Glenn
*Editor*: Tony Lawson
*Music*: Stanley Myers
*Songs*: 'M.O.T.H.E.R.' by Morse, O'Hara; 'Mother' by Lennon; 'When the Red Red Robin Comes Bob Bob Bobbin' Along' by Woods; 'Chattanooga Choo Choo' by Warren, Gordon; 'Young at Heart' by Richards, Leigh, performed by Rosemary Clooney
*Film Extract*: Cape Fear (1961)
*Cast*: Theresa Russell (*Linda Henry*), Gary Oldman (*Martin/fairground man*), Christopher Lloyd (*Dr Henry Henry*), Colleen Camp (*Arlanda*), Sandra Bernhard (Nurse Stein), Seymour Cassel (*Dr Bernard Fairmont*), Leon Rippy (*trucker*), Vance Colvig (*Mr Ennis*), Kathryn Tomlinson (*receptionist*), Jerry Rushing (*redneck*), Tommy Hull (*counterman*), J. Michael Hunter (*waiter*), Richard K. Olsen (*delegate*), Ted Barrow (*old man*)
90 minutes, colour

## 1992
### Secret Friends
UK; A Whistling Gypsy Production presented by Film Four International and Robert Michael Geisler, John Roberdeau, based on the novel *Ticket to Ride* by Dennis Potter
*Executive producers*: Robert Michael Geisler, John Roberdeau
*Producer*: Rosemarie Whitman
*Associate producer*: Alison Barnett
*Director*: Dennis Potter
*Production designer*: Gary Williamson
*Cinematography*: Sue Gibson
*Editor*: Clare Douglas
*Music*: Nicholas Russell-Pavier
*Sound*: Andrew Glen
*Cast*: Alan Bates (*John*), Gina Bellman (*Helen*), Frances Barber (*Angela*), Tony Doyle (*Martin*), Joanna David (*Kate*), Colin Jeavons (*vicar*), Rowena Cooper (*vicar's wife*), Ian McNeice (*first businessman*), Davyd Harries (*second businessman*), Martin Whiting (*young John*), Niven Boyd (*BR steward/patient*), Roy Hamilton (*singer*), Nicholas Russell-Pavier, Colin Ryan, David Swift (*musicians*)
97 minutes, colour

# Bibliography

## BOOKS BY DENNIS POTTER

### Non-fiction

*The Glittering Coffin* (1960, Gollancz)
*The Changing Forest: Life in the Forest of Dean Today* (1962, Secker and Warburg)

### Fiction

*Hide and Seek* (1973, André Deutsch/Quartet Books; reissued by Faber and Faber)
*Pennies from Heaven* (1981, Quartet Books)
*Ticket to Ride* (1986, Faber and Faber)
*Blackeyes* (1987, Faber and Faber)

### Published plays

*The Nigel Barton Plays: Two Television Plays* (1967, Penguin)
*Son of Man* (1970, André Deutsch)
*Follow the Yellow Brick Road* (in *The Television Dramatist*, 1973, Elek)
*Brimstone and Treacle* (1978, Eyre Methuen)
*Sufficient Carbohydrate* (1983, Faber and Faber)
*Waiting for the Boat, On Television: Blue Remembered Hills, Joe's Ark, Cream in my Coffee* (1984, Faber and Faber)
*The Singing Detective* (1986, Faber and Faber)
*Lipstick on your Collar* (1993, Faber and Faber)

## SELECTED INTERVIEWS AND ARTICLES

Barker, Adam, 'What the Detective Saw' (on *Track 29*), *Monthly Film Bulletin*, vol. 55, no. 654, July 1988, pp. 193–5
Canby, Vincent, 'Is the Year's Best Film on TV?' (on *The Singing Detective*), *New York Times (Arts & Leisure section)*, 10 July 1988
Cunningham, John, 'Flavour of Decay' (on *Sufficient Carbohydrate*), *Guardian*, 6 December 1983
Dougary, Ginny, 'Potter's Weal', *The Times Saturday Review*, 26 September 1992, pp. 4–10
Fiddick, Peter, 'Counting the Pennies' (on the LWT deal), *Guardian*, 29 July 1980

– 'The Careful Cultivator' (on *Cream in my Coffee*), *Guardian*, 3 November 1980

Fuller, Graham, 'Dennis in Fatherland' (on *Christabel*), *Village Voice*, 21 February 1989, p. 55

– 'Dollars from Heaven', *Listener*, vol. 121, no. 3112, 4 May 1989, p. 33–4

Hoberman, J., 'Noir Out' (on *The Singing Detective*), *Village Voice*, 13 December 1988, p. 73

Hunt, Albert, 'Plays Portentous' (on *Blade on the Feather, Rain on the Roof, Cream in my Coffee*), *New Society*, 11 June 1980

Koenig, Rhoda, 'The Pain of a Black Eye from the Critics' (on *Blackeyes*, serial), *Independent*, 18 December 1989

Lichtenstein, Therese, 'Syncopated Thriller: Dennis Potter's *Singing Detective*', *Artforum*, vol. 28, no. 9, May 1990, pp. 168–72

Saynor, James, 'Black and Blue' (*Blackeyes* production story), *Listener*, vol. 121, no. 3116, 1 June 1989, pp. 4–7

– 'What Every Woman Knows' (on *Blackeyes*, serial), *Listener*, vol. 122, no. 3143, 7 December 1989, pp. 46–7

Taubin, Amy, 'Potter's Field of *Cream*' (on *Cream in my Coffee*), *Village Voice*, 20 February 1990, p. 57

Ward, Alex, 'TV's Tormented Master', *New York Times Magazine*, 13 November 1988, pp. 38–41, 86–90

Wyver, John, 'Paradise Perhaps' (on *Pennies from Heaven*, serial), *Time Out*, 3 March 1978, pp. 12–13

– 'The Long Non-Revolution of Dennis Potter' (on *Blade on the Feather*), 17 October 1980, pp. 18–19

– 'Arrows of Desire' (on *Blackeyes*, serial), *New Statesman and Society*, 24 November 1989, pp. 16–19

# A note on the editor

Graham Fuller is Executive Editor of *Interview* magazine in New York. He previously worked as Executive Editor of *The Movie* and *The History of Rock*, as Editor of *Unsolved*, and as Films Editor at *Stills* and American *Elle*. He has written on film and television for *Projections*, the *Listener*, *Sight and Sound*, the *Guardian*, *The Times*, the *Independent*, *Village Voice*, *Film Comment* and *American Film*.

# Index

*Page numbers in italics
refer to illustrations*

*Adventures of Robin Hood, The*, 103
Albery Theatre, London, 107
*Alice*: reworking, x, 28, 106; 'splashing water' scene, 28–9; theme, xiv; writing, 28
*Alice in Wonderland*, 119
Allen, Jim, 15, 18, 115
Amiel, Jon, 92–3, 95
Amis, Martin, 128
Andrews, Dana, 8
*Angels Are So Few*: images, 128; performances, 122; themes, xiv, 48; title, 91; used in *Only Make Believe*, 47–8; visitation motif, 16, 40
Apted, Michael, 106
*Arena*, 11
Ashcroft, Peggy, *61*

Badel, Alan, *53*
Bailey, John, 27
Banks, Iain, 128
Barber, Frances, 127
Barnes, Julian, xiv
Barr, Patrick, *35*
Barrie, J.M., 119
Barron, Keith, 17
Bates, Alan, 66, 126, 137, *135*, *136*
BBC: bans *Brimstone and Treacle*, 17–18n, 58; documentaries, 2, 3, 11; drama, 15, 18, 32, 33, 106; *Pennies from Heaven* rights, 58, 105; Potter's career, 3, 11; *Tender is the Night*, 74; *Vote, Vote, Vote for Nigel Barton* transmission, 17, 31
*Beast with Two Backs, A*: cruelty, 55; filming, 36; Forest of Dean setting, 1, 16, 34, 70; plot, 34–6; *35*
Bell, Tom, 122
Bellman, Gina, 126, 132, *129*, *136*
*Between Two Rivers*, 2, 3, 11, 23
Bevan, Aneurin, 13
Bielenberg, Christabel (*née* Burton), 66–7, 75–9
Bielenberg, Peter, 67, 76–7

Bird, John, *57*
*Blackeyes*: character of Jessica, xiv, 17, 127; complexity, 121; direction, xvii, 33, 125–6, 134, 139; 'doubled' character, 17; filming, 125; narrative, 126; Potter as narrator, 126, 132–3; quoted, 125; reception, xvi, 64, 125–6, 133, 139; structure, 81; themes, 2, 46, 106, 130–1, 137; writing, 128–32; *129*, *131*
*Blade on the Feather*: betrayal theme, 43, 45; budget, 18; characters, 43, 45; direction, 105; making, 58; reworking, xv; song, 91–2; visitation motif, 16; *44*
Blake, William, 42
Blakeley, Colin, 17, *39*
*Blue Remembered Hills*: adults as children, 31, 55–8; cruelty, 55; direction, 105; Forest of Dean setting, 1; Potter's satisfaction with, 141; 'surprise element', 64; *57*
Blunt, Anthony, 16, 43
Bochko, Steve, 80
*Bonegrinder, The*: expression of prejudice, 34; Rediffusion, 17, 33: theme, xiv, 108
*Bookstand*, 11
Borges, Jorge Luis, 86
Bowie, David, 106
Bowlly, Al, xiv, 37, 84, *85*
Briarpatch Film Corporation, 125n
Bridges, Alan, 59
*Brimstone and Treacle*: banned, 17, 52; film, 105, 113; novel, 4; performances, 122; politics, 21, 50–1, 105; staged, 107; visitation motif, 16, 40–1, 50–2
Browne, Sam, 85
Browne, Coral, *118*
Burgess, Guy, 43

Caine, Hall, 5
Campbell, Cheryl, 59, 81, 105, *90*
Canby, Vincent, xvii
Carroll, Lewis, *see* Dodgson
*Casanova*, 64, 68–70, 82, *69*

Casanova, Giacomo, 65, 68, 70
*Cathy Come Home*, 15
CBS, 80
Channel 4, xvi, 18, 31, 81, 125
Chelsom, Peter, 61
*Christabel*: Alice reference, 119;
   development, 76–9, 92; origins, 66–7,
   75–6; reviews, 64; Trodd's involvement
   18, 66; *78*
Churchill, Winston, 17, 25, 31
*Cinderella*, 32, 33
Coleridge, Samuel Taylor, 21
*Commune, The*, 18
*Confidence Course, The*: development, 3,
   15, 19; reception, 17; visitation motif,
   16; wiped, 18; 20
Conservative Party, 12, 21, 42
Constable, John, 42
Conti, Tom, 45, 44
*Cop Rock*, 80, 85, 111
Corliss, Richard, xvii
*Count of Monte Cristo, The*, 8, *9*
Coward, Noël, 84
Cowgill, Bryan, 17n
Craven, Gemma, 80
*Cream in my Coffee*: budget, 18; direction,
   105; making, 58; song, 91; themes,
   59–60; *61, 62*
Crisp, Quentin, 18n
Cropper, Anna, *123*
Crucible Theatre, Sheffield, 107
Curry, Tim, *123*

*Daily Herald*, 3, 10–12, 14, 19, 141
Dale Carnegie Institute, 17, 19
*Dance to the Music of Time, A*, 18
Darwin, Charles, 54
Davies, Gareth, 32
Davis, Barry, 17n
*Diary of a Young Man*, 15
Dickens, Charles, 107, 128
Dillon, Stephen, 67, *78*
Dobie, Alan, 16
Dodgson, Charles Lutwidge (Lewis
   Carroll) 28, 67, 116, 119
Doré, Edna, 67
Dors, Diana, 98
*Double Dare*: characters, 46; direction,
   105; 'doubled' character, 17, 113, 126;
   script, 112–13; themes, 16–17, 50; title,
   91
Doyle, Tony, 127
*Dreamchild*: 'doubled' character, 17;
   impact, xiv; making, 121 reworking,
   xv, 28, 106; US showing, xvii; writing,
   28, 116–19; *118, 120*
Duvitski, Janine, *57*

D.W. Griffith Award, xvii

Eden, Anthony, 103
Eliot, T.S., 38, 109, 128
Elliott, Denholm, 16, 21
Ellis, Robin, *57*
Elphick, Michael, *57*
*Emergency – Ward 9*, 18
*Encore*, 15

Film on Four series, xvi, 18
Finlay, Frank, 65, *69*
Fitzgerald, Ella, xiii
Fitzgerald, F. Scott, 64–5, 72
Fitzgerald, Zelda, 65
*Follow the Yellow Brick Road*: characters,
   46, 47; images, 128; psychotherapy, 37;
   quoted, 15; theme, 16, 34, 47
Ford, John, 1
Forest of Dean, 1, 4–5, 7, 16, 34, 37, 38,
   66
Freud, Sigmund, 28–9

Gambon, Michael, 81, *94*
Garnett, Tony, 15
Germaine, Louise, 81, 101, *100*
Gibson, Brian, 105
*Glittering Coffin, The*, 2
Goldie, Grace Wyndham, 3
*Gorky Park*, 106, 113–15, *114*
Gosse, Edmund, 5, 52–5
Gosse, Philip, 54–5
Gough, Michael, 126, *131*
Grade, Michael, 18, 125n
*Great Gatsby, The*, 71–2
Greene, Richard, 103
Griffiths, Trevor, 15

Hammersmith, 1, 7–8
Hardy, Thomas, 34, 48, 66, 70, 128
Hargreaves, Alice, 119, *118*
Harris, Max, *53*
Hartley, L.P., 79
Haymes, Dick, 8
Hazlitt, William, xiii, xvi, 19–21
Hedley, Jack, *44*
Henshall, Douglas, *83*
Henson, Jim, 116
*Hide and Seek*, 2, 127
Hoffman, Dustin, 107
Hopcraft, Arthur, 64
Hopkins, John, 15
Hoskins, Bob, 80, 105, *89*
Housman, A.E., 56
Hudd, Roy, 82
Hume, Basil, 48
Hunt, Holman, 38

Hurley, Elizabeth, 67, *78*
Hurt, William, 106, 113, *114*

Ink Spots, the, xiii
Interart Theater, 107
'Into Each Life Some Rain Must Fall', xiii
'It Might as Well be Spring', 8

Jeavons, Colin, *57*
Jeffries, Lionel, *61*
Jhabvala, Ruth Prawer, 71
*Joe's Ark*: themes, 48–9; visitation motif, 16, 48
Joffé, Roland, 18
Johnson, Samuel, 21

Kael, Pauline, 106
Kaye, Nora, 112
Keats, John, 71
Kennedy Martin, Troy, 15
Kierkegaard, Sören, 41
Kitchen, Michael, 122

Labour Party, 13–14, 17, 31
Lansing, Sherry, 112
*Late Call*, 65–6, 67–8, 82
*Lay Down Your Arms*: father character, 5; LWT, 17; reworking, xv, 97; Suez crisis, 10, 97
Le Carré, John, 16
Le Mesurier, John, *42*, *44*
Lennon, Peter, 64
Lewis, Jerry Lee, 98
Liddell, Alice, 28, 116, 119
*Lipstick on your Collar*: budget, 97; characters, 97, 98–101; direction, 31, 97, 125; expectations, xvi; fantasy, 104; mood, 104; narrative, 81–2, 102; origins, 125n; Potter's satisfaction with, 141; production, 139–40; quoted, 139; reworking, xv; songs, 29, 80, 82, 97–8, 101, 103; Suez crisis, 10, 101–3; teen years, 10; *83*, *99*, *100*
Lisemore, Martin, 66
Loach, Ken, 15
Loncraine, Richard, *105*
London Weekend Television (LWT), xvii, 18, 33, 58, 115, 125
Lyell, Sir Charles, 54

McCallum, Rick, *125*
McGrath, John, 15
McGregor, Ewan, 82, 103, *83*, *100*
Mackenzie, John, 105
Maclean, Donald, 43
McLeod, Shelagh, *61*
Macmillan, Harold, 82

Major, John, 25
Markham, Kika, 17
Martin, Steve, 105, *110*
Marvin, Lee, 106
Maw, Janet, 66
Maynard, Bill, 12
*Mayor of Casterbridge, The*, 34, 64, 66, 70–1
Mercer, David, 2, 15
*Mesmer*, 106, 113, 124
Mesmer, Franz Anton, 106, 124
*Message for Posterity*: reception, 17; style, 31–2; theme, xiv, 25–6; wiped, 18
MGM, 105, 109–12
*Midnight Movie*, 106, 124
Millar, Gavin, 105, *120*
Milne, Alasdair, 17, 17–18n, 52
Mirren, Helen, *57*
Mitchell, Denis, 3
*Moonlight on the Highway*: making, 17; psychotherapy, 37; songs, 84; themes, xiv, 2, 37; title, 91; Trodd's involvement, 18; visitation motif, 16
Morgan, Margaret, *see* Potter
Murdoch, Rupert, 140
Museum of Television and Radio, New York, xiii
*Mystery of Edwin Drood, The*, 107

Nasser, Gamal Abdel, 103
Nathan, David, 11
National Front, 21, 51, 105
New College, Oxford, 2
New Left, 13
*New Statesman*, 2, 3, 18n
New York Film Critics' Circle, xvii
Nichols, Dandy, 65
Northcliffe, Lord, 66

Oldman, Gary, 122, *123*
*Only Make Believe*: staged, 107; themes, 48, 50; title, 91; use of *Angels Are So Few*, 47–8; visitation motif, 16, 38
Orion, 106
Orwell, George, 6, 19–21, 45
Owen, Alun, 2

*Panorama*, 3
*Paper Roses*: character of Hubbard, 12; Granada, 17; themes, xiv, 12, 34
Papp, Joseph, xvii
*Past is Myself, The*, 66, 75
PBS, xvii
*Pennies from Heaven*: casting, 59; character of Arthur Parker, 25, 75, 82–4, 86, 87–91, 106, *89*, *110*; development, 18; 'doubled' character, 17; film, 105–6, 108–12; Forest of Dean

setting, 1; length, 121; music, 7; plot,
80–1; Potter's satisfaction with, 141;
quoted, 105; reputation, xvi, 64; rights,
58, 105; songs, 16, 25, 29, 31, 80–1,
84–5, 86, 87, 92, 98, 103; structure,
82; 'surprise element', 64; Trodd's
attitude, 31; visitation motif, 16; *89,
90, 110*
Peters, Bernadette, 105
P.F.H. Ltd, 18
*Phantom of the Opera*, 124
Phelan, Brian, 18n
Philby, Kim, 16, 31, 43, 45
Pinter, Harold, 106
Planer, Nigel, 126
Plater, Alan, 64
Platters, the, 98
Play for Today series, 15, 17n, 121
Pleasence, Donald, *44*
Potter, Dennis: autobiographical forms,
10, 96; BBC career, 3, 11; childhood,
1–2, 4–8; cinema influences, 7–8;
directing, xvii, 33, 97, 106, 125–6,
134–7, 139; dramatizations, 64–79;
education, 2–3, 4–6; Forest of Dean, 1,
2n, 4–5, 37; Hollywood, 18, 105–16;
illness, xiii, 3, 10–11, 12–13, 14, 32–3,
96, 125, 134, 139; journalism, 3,
11–12; marriage, 3–4; media, xvi–xvii,
93–4, 105, 121–2; misogyny
accusations, 133, 137; National Service,
10, 102; non-naturalism, xv, 15, 30–1,
64; novels, xvi, 46, 92, 125, 127–8; on
autobiography, 10; on guilt, 23–4; on
identity, 22–3, 60; on nostalgia, 22, 96,
101–2; on psychoanalysis, 28–9, 37–8,
56; on self (real and invented), 10–11;
optimism, xv, 46, 48, 140; politics, 3,
13–14, 21, 24; relationship with BBC,
15, 17–18, 32, 33, 58; religion, xiv, 4–5,
7, 19, 38–42, 47–9; stage plays, 107;
television criticism, 3; use of songs, 16,
25, 29, 31, 80–104; writing process,
26–9, 140–1; THEMES: American
culture, 108; authors, xv, 46–8, 50;
betrayal, xiv, 2, 42–6, 56, 60; child
abuse, 2, 37, 55; childhood, 55–6;
class, xv, 2–3, 43, 81; commerciality of
sex, 130–1, 137–8; 'doubled'
characters, 17, 113, 126; English
condition, xiv, 5, 16, 42–3, 103; fathers
and sons, 3, 5, 23–4, 54–5; Forest of
Dean setting, 1, 16, 34, 70; guilt, xiv,
23–4; identity quest, xiv, 60, 65, 81;
Oedipal, 28–9, 59, 122; politics, xiv,
16, 17, 24–6, 51; popular culture, xiv,
29; psychotherapy, xiii, 37, 56;

religion, 38–42, 51–5; sexual disgust,
xiv, xv, 133; sexual inhibition, xiv, 48,
137; sovereign self, 60, 81; visitation
motif, 16, 38, 40–2, 48, 50–2, 59
Potter, Jane (daughter), 4
Potter, June (sister), 1
Potter, Margaret (mother), 1, 3, 6–7
Potter, Margaret (*née* Morgan, wife), 3–4
Potter, Robert (son), 4
Potter, Sarah (daughter), 4
Potter, Walter (father), 1, 3, 5–6
Powell, Anthony, 18
Powell, Jonathan, 66, 93
Presley, Elvis, 98
Price, Dennis, 20
Public Theater, xvii
*Pushkin*, 124
Pushkin, Alexander, 72, 82

*Rain on the Roof*: budget, 18; casting, 59;
making, 58; themes, xv, 10, 59;
visitation motif, 16
Ransome, Arthur, 71
*Rapunzel*, 119
Rediffusion, 33
Reynolds, Lance, 106
*Reynolds News*, 2
Rickman, Alan, 106
Rodgers and Hammerstein, 8
Roeg, Nicolas, 106, 122, 134
Ross, Herbert, 18, 105, 106, 111, 112
Rossington, Norman, 65
Round House, London, 107
Royle, Carol, 126
Ruskin, John, 119
Russell, Theresa, 122, *123*
Rye, Renny, 82, 97, 106, 125n, *100*

Sandford, Jeremy, 15
Sarris, Andrew, xvii
Saynor, James, 65n
*Schmoedipus*: development, 28–9;
reworking, xv, 106, 122; visitation
motif, 16, 40; *123*
Screen One, 18
Screen Two, 18
*Secret Friends*: character of John, 137;
direction, 33, 106, 126, 134–7, 139;
'doubled' character, 17, 126; father
character, 5; narrative, 126–7; origins,
125; production, 125n; reception, 126,
139; structure, 93; style, xvi; theme,
106, 137–8; visitation motif, 16; *135,
136*
Seven Network, 74
*Shaggy Dog*: LWT, 17, 33; theme, xiv, 34;
wiped, 18
Shankley, Amelia, *118*

Shaw, Martin, 62
Shivas, Mark, 134
Showtime, 74
Simenon, Georges, 70
Sinfield, Alan, 2
Singing Detective, The: autobiographical
assumptions, 10, 50, 95–6; betrayal,
56; character of Philip Marlow, 25, 127;
'doubled' character, 17; fantasy, 97;
father character, 3; filming, 93–5; Forest
of Dean setting, 1; images, 128;
influence, 106; length, 121; London, 7;
mood, 91; plot, 81; Potter's response,
xiii; Potter's satisfaction with, 141;
psychotherapy, xiii, 37, 56; quoted,
xvi, 1, 80; reputation, xvi, 64; rewriting,
92–3; songs, 29, 86–7, 91, 92, 96, 98,
103; structure, 81, 82, 87, 91, 93, 111;
themes, xv, 2, 50, 65; US reception,
xvii, 96; US film version, 107; 94
Smith, Martin Cruz, 106
Son of Man: agnosticism, 38; Christ figure,
40; making, 40; theme, 16; reception,
17; staged, 107; 39
Spottiswoode, Roger, 106
Stalin, Joseph, 43
Stallybrass, Anne, 66
Stand Up, Nigel Barton: absolution, 23–4;
adults as children, 55, 85; betrayal, 2,
46, 56; father character, 5, 23–4; stage
version, 107; style, 30; themes, xiv, 2,
3, 46; transmission, 17
Stargazers, the, 82, 102
State Fair, 8, 9
Steenburgen, Mary, 64
Stevenson, Robert Louis, 66
Sting, 113
Strauss, Peter, 64, 73
Sufficient Carbohydrate, 10, 18, 107, 108
Sun, 3, 14
Sunday Times, 3

Tarzan, 8
Tender is the Night, 64, 72–4, 73
That Was the Week That Was, 11
Thatcher, Margaret, 25
Theatre Royal, Bristol, 107
Thomas, D.M., 106
Thomas, Giles, 81, 103, 83, 99
Ticket to Ride, 125, 127
Times, The, 68
Tolkien, J.R.R., 16

Tolstoy, Leo, 128
Toto le héros, 106
Track 29: attitude to US, 108; direction,
106, 122; reworking, xv, 122; 123
Tragedy of Two Ambitions, A, 34, 70
Traitor: father character, 5: Philby
character, 16, 31, 45; theme, xiv, 16,
42–3; 44
Trodd, Kenith: BBC relationship 17–18;
Blackeyes, 125; Blue Remembered
Hills casting, 31; Brimstone and Treacle,
105; LWT contract, 18; NY Potter
seminar, xiii; on Potter's television
writing, xiv; Pennies from Heaven
response, 31; relationship with Potter,
125; Singing Detective, 125; 120
Trollope, Anthony, 128
20th Century-Fox, 74, 106, 112

Unexpected Valleys, 106, 112

Van Dormael, Jaco, 106
Vaughan, Frankie, 82
Visitors, 18, 48, 108
Vote, Vote, Vote for Nigel Barton:
alterations, 17; Bevan footage, 13;
staged, 107; style, 30; theme xiv, 16, 25;
transmission, 17, 31; 27

Waiting for the Boat, 2
Walken, Christopher, 110
Walker, Polly, 106
Wasp Factory, The, 128
Wednesday Play series, 15, 31, 121
Welland, Colin, 55–6, 57
Wesker, Arnold, 2
Where Adam Stood: child abuse, 2, 55;
father character, 5, 54–5; Father and
Son, 52; Potter's satisfaction with, 141;
religious fundamentalism, 54–5; 53
Where the Buffalo Roam, xiv, 8–10, 59
Whistling Gypsy, 106, 125n
White Hotel, The, 106
Whitehouse, Mary, 65
Whitelaw, Billie, 16
Whitman, Rosemarie, 125n
Wilson, Angus, 65
Wizard of Oz, The, 116, 119, 117
Wordsworth, William, 21

Yentob, Alan, 11, 105